Crimes of the Powerful

CRIMES OF

Frank Pearce

THE POWERFUL

Marxism, Crime and Deviance

Foreword by Jock Young

Pluto **Press**

HV
6791
P4
1976

First published 1976 by Pluto Press Limited
Unit 10 Spencer Court, 7 Chalcot Road, London NW1 8LH
Copyright © Pluto Press 1976
ISBN 0 904383 05 9
Printed in Great Britain by Robert MacLehose & Co Ltd,
Glasgow and typeset by V. Siviter Smith & Co Ltd, Birmingham
Designed by Richard Hollis, GrR
Cover picture: from the film *Black Legion* 1937,
courtesy of Warner Brothers

Contents

Part 3: Organised Crime in Historical Context

Acknowledgements

For the opportunity to exchange ideas, for emotional support, for typing and for criticism I am grateful to: Tony Woodiwiss, Harold Wolpe, Mike Hayes, Colin Prescod, Tony Bunyan, Nigel Williams, Jock Young, Paul Walton, Ian Taylor, Jerry Palmer, Glenn Goodwin, Joe Albini, Mary McIntosh, Graham Packham, Paula Struhl, Karsten Struhl, John Dennington, Andy Roberts, Jane Bowden, Colin Low, Mike Gonzalez, Stefan Ronay, Mike Brake, Paul Zeal, Lesley Corner, Rita Brown, Matt Connelly, Rick Kuper and Linda Pearce.

To my comrades in the struggle
to democratise the Polytechnic of North London

Foreword

The textbooks on criminology like to advance the idea that prisoners are mentally defective. There is only the merest suggestion that the system itself is at fault. Penologists regard prisons as asylums . . . But what can we say about these asylums since *none* of the inmates are ever cured. Since in every instance they are sent out of the prison more damaged physically and mentally than when they entered. Because that is the reality. Do you continue to investigate the inmate? Where does administrative responsibility begin? Perhaps the administration of the prison cannot be held accountable for every individual act of their charges, but when things fly apart along racial lines, when the breakdown can be traced so clearly to circumstances even beyond the control of the guards and administration, investigation of anything outside of the tenets of the fascist system itself is futile.[1]

George Jackson writing in his Soledad cell captures in a few sentences a position which academic criminology has only recently and with great labour arrived at. For it is not the criminal nor even the administration of crime but, in the final analysis, the system itself that must be investigated.

To understand the significance of Frank Pearce's book on crime and the American state it is necessary to summarise briefly the profound changes that have occurred within criminology over the last decade. For over this short period the subject has been transformed from parodying the most conventional prejudices of bourgeois society to becoming a significant cockpit of theoretical debate.

It is to American deviancy theory of the 1960s that we owe the first concerted attempts to demolish the accepted paradigm in which crime and social intransigence had been viewed throughout the century. Pivotal works in this endeavour were Howard Becker's *Outsiders*[2] and David Matza's *Becoming Deviant*.[3] Their critique was of correctional criminology, the type of theory which had unswervingly identified itself with the interests of the powerful. The criminal was portrayed as suffering from a lack of socialisation arising out of either a genetic inability to become fully human or an environmental influence which had impaired his social development. The social world itself was envisaged as a taken-for-granted consensus where all *adequate* men and women agreed on the essential fairness and rationality of their society. To steal, to be gay, to smoke marihuana, to engage in acts of violence – all these activities were viewed as indicative of a fundamental malaise of the individual involved. The task of the correctional criminologist was then characterised in a progressive light, for, whereas conservative law-and-order campaigns would call for severer punishment of the offender, the 'scientific' expert would advise on the appropriate diagnosis and treatment of the culprit. He would then deal with the irrational compulsions which propel the criminal or deviant into his anti-social actions. From the view of schizophrenics as suffering from a biochemical disorder, to the drug treatment programmes inflicted on Californian criminals, to the labelling of Soviet dissidents as mentally ill, such correctional or positivistic conceptions of deviance were until the 1960s relatively unchallenged.

The new wave of deviancy theorists trenchantly dismissed such notions. A satisfactory explanation of criminal action, they argued, needed to answer two questions: why did the individual wish to commit the crime, and why was the action considered criminal or deviant in the first place? Correctional criminology had mystified both answers: the first by taking from the criminal any sense of human purpose, the second by totally ignoring the problem of social reaction. The reasons for criminality were reduced to non-human, material factors of either the person's inner physiology or his social environment which impelled him into crime. To counter the first answer, the new deviancy theorists demanded a fully human actor: a person whose choice, whose deviancy is understandable and comprehensible in terms of his moral career through the social world. To counter the second, they noted how correctional criminology had achieved an outstanding feat. For it had managed to discuss crime for nearly a century without recourse to a theory of the state. The reaction against crime was taken for granted; it did not need an explanation because all decent-minded men were in agreement as to its anti-social nature.

It was at this juncture that the new deviancy theorists introduced their most characteristic concept: *labelling*. Society, they argued, did not consist of a monolithic consensus but rather of a pluralistic array of values. For an action to be termed criminal or deviant demanded two activities: one, that of a group or individual acting in a particular fashion, the other, that of another group or individual with different values labelling the initial activity as deviant. Human beings acting creatively in the world constantly generated their own system of values. Unfortunately within the pluralistic order of society certain groups – variously and vaguely termed 'the powerful', 'the bureaucracy', 'the moral entrepreneur' – having more power than others, *enforced* their values upon the less powerful, labelling those who infringed their rules with stereotypical tags. That is, man, who in fact, was existentially free to evolve any values he chose, or experiment with various forms of behaviour, became labelled by the authorities as *in essence* 'a homosexual', 'a thief', or 'a psychopath'. Moreover, this very act of labelling, by limiting the future choices of the actor and by being presented to the actor as being the truth about his nature, with all the force of authority, had a self-fulfilling effect. The old adages: 'once a thief always a thief', 'once a junkie always a junkie', *became* true not because, as earlier criminologists had maintained, this was the essence of the man involved but because the power of labelling transformed and cajoled men into acting and believing *as if* they possessed no freedom in the world.

Ironically, however incisive this analysis of correctional criminology was on a preliminary level and however important its insights, the conception of human nature and social order held by these deviancy theorists was inadequate to carry the weight of their criticism. By granting man freedom in an absolute sense without acknowledging any material constraints human purpose was reduced to the level of whimsy. By characterising society as a simple diversity of values, they blinded themselves to the existence of a very real consensus – the hegemonic domination of bourgeois values. By pointing to power without analysing its class basis and the nature of the state, they transformed the actions of the powerful into an arbitrary flexing of moral muscles. In this fashion, a vulgar materialist criminology which caricatured the criminal as determined by non-purposive material factors was *inverted* to become an idealist criminology where crime was a product of men purposively pursuing ideas detached and free from material circumstances.

The new deviancy theorists castigated correctional criminology for being ideological. By arguing that all activity which threatened the interests of the powerful was not purposive but merely the non-rational result of under-socialisation, the vulgar materialists safeguarded subtly the notion of society as harmonious and just. But the idealists, themselves, evolved their own ideology. For by propounding a conception of man as free and spontaneous before the intervention of the state sullied and transformed his freedom, they threw all the weight of their criticism on bad administration. It was a romantic theory of the noble deviant, expressive and creative, who was bowed under the fetters of state control.

Thus whereas materialist theory, however distortedly, had emphasised the make-up of the individual and the structure of his social arrangements as generating deviancy and had ignored the effects of state action, idealist theory accomplished precisely the reverse. Criminology admitted that crime was a product of the psychology or the social circumstances of the individual 'going wrong', though it was careful to dissociate this from any denunciation of the existing order. Idealist theory romantically suggested that nothing was wrong with the structure of society and the individual psyche outside of the maladministration of the state and heavy-handed central agencies. A precise parallel to this is where liberal 'enlightened' commentators on industrial affairs view strikes not as a result of the fundamental irrationality of workers – as more conservative observers would have it – but as the outcome of mismanagement, of unwise decisions in the sphere of labour relations. In this manner the underlying conflict endemic to a class society is perfunctorily glossed over.

The task of a marxist criminology is to move beyond this oscillation between vulgar materialism and idealism which is so characteristic of bourgeois thought. Central to our concern is the explanation of law and criminality in terms of the dominant mode of production and the class nature of society. Man is seen both as a product of circumstances beyond his control and as an historical actor potentially capable of transforming these circumstances. The working-class criminal is a man beset by material circumstances, existing in a social world where the sanctity of property and desirability of existing forms of behaviour are incessantly proclaimed whether it be in the school, the media or the workplace. He, within his own subculture, attempts to

14

overcome his predicament albeit falteringly and with an inarticulate consciousness. That the 'delinquent solution' is no real solution, that it often merely exacerbates his own plight and that of his fellows, is obvious. It is only romantics – and many of the idealists merged into this category – who could view the petty thief, the violent offender and even the schizophrenic, as in some way acting authentically in their circumstances. For to grant an actor purposiveness and consciousness is not to say that his solution is tenable, nor to condone his actions, nor to agree with his assessment of his predicament.

At this juncture a number of writers, amongst whom Paul Hirst has been the most prominent, have argued that the criminal is not a legitimate subject for marxist analysis.[4] Carefully selecting his texts he notes how the criminal is a member of the lumpenproletariat: 'the social scum' easily beguiled into becoming the 'bribed tool of a reactionary clique'. As a parasitic group living off productive labour its class interests are diametrically opposed to those of the workers. Further, crime and deviancy are endemic to all societies whether socialist or capitalist. Thus he writes: 'One cannot imagine the absence of the control of traffic or the absence of the suppression of theft and murder, nor can one consider these controls as purely oppressive.'[5] The criminal enterprise is not only marginal to the capitalist system, it is a continuing problem to be faced in all societies. From this perspective a marxist criminology is stillborn, a theoretical product tainted with revisionist premises, unimportant to a socialist analysis. What can be said against these charges?

1. Crime and the Ruling Class

Ruling class crime and illegal business activities, political illegalities and police malpractices are endemic in capitalist societies. They are directly involved in the extraction of surplus value. A central problematic for a marxist theory of the state is: why are the rulemakers the most extravagant rulebreakers? Pearce confronts this problem in detail indicating precisely the fallacious nature of the notion that crime is a marginal phenomenon to the capitalist system. Al Capone was not only a major innovator in the integration and diversification of the

15

crime industry in America, he was also amazingly insightful as to the hypocrisy of the powerful. 'Business', he once sneered, 'those are the legitimate rackets . . . They talk about me not being on the legitimate. Nobody's on the legit. You know that and so do they.' In a decade of Watergate and Poulson there is little more that one can add to this.

2. Organised Crime and Big Business

Big business, particularly in the American context of this book, has never been loath to use professional criminal help when it was needed, whether it has involved the control of unions or industrial espionage. Politicians, likewise, have frequently developed close ties with organised crime and many an election has been carried by a political machine underpinned by criminal organisations. Capone may have been exaggerating when he said: 'Why the biggest bankers and businessmen and politicians and professional men are looking to me to keep the system going', but the evidence for organised criminal involvement in the social control apparatus is widespread. Thus there is criminal involvement in the maintenance of the extraction of surplus value; and organised crime, like the police force – which Hirst readily admits as a proper object of study – must be understood in this context.

Further, organised crime at a certain stage of its development inevitably moves into legitimate business areas. Thus the capital built up during the Prohibition period was ploughed back into trucking companies, dairies, launderette chains, real estate and supermarkets. Moreover, many unions were enmeshed in its control – the International Longshoremen's Association, the Teamsters, and the Union of Operating Engineers, to name a few. Thus the distinction between legitimate and illegitimate enterprises is, in many cases, blurred.

3. Crime and Socialist Strategy

Quite aside from the degree to which organised crime is involved in productive relationships, the questions of crime in the corporations, crime in the police, crime in the unions,

16

and crime in the streets are central concerns in terms of socialist strategy. The exposé of how the bourgeoisie wilfully break their own rules is a useful demonstrating in demonstating the true nature of civil society. Crime in the unions and corruption in the labour movement must be, as Pearce indicates, fought on a socialist platform. Crime in the streets is a real problem for working-class communities. The control of crime, like the control of ratebusting in the factory, is a concern of socialists whether it is countering conservative law-and-order campaigns in American cities,[6] or eliminating anti-socialist activities in pre-revolutionary Algeria.

4.   Crime and Ideology

The whole gist of Hirst's argument against a marxist criminology is based on a further glaring omission. It ignores the ideological function of law and the punishment of the criminal. The dominant ideology of capitalist society insists that the interests of the bourgeoisie are the national interest, that exploitation is, in fact, a fair return for a fair day's work, that the chaos of civil society is harmony, that an unjust society is one of justice, equality and tolerance. To maintain a pliant and placid work force demands a continuous enforcement of work discipline. Thus members of the working class, from school to factory, are subject to a lifetime of control based on rewards and punishments. The good worker – the company man – is extolled and promoted; the malcontent – the troublemaker – given the worst jobs, lowest rate of pay or laid off. The ideology learnt, in this fashion, in the workplace is detailed and elaborated in the mass media. Law is seen as an instrument for the adjustment of social justice: for ensuring that the rewards of hard work, property and possessions, are protected and the rule violators duly punished. Just as the population must be convinced that utility to society is proportionally rewarded, they must also be made aware that lack of utility is effectively curbed and stigmatised. The pyramid of success must have a shadow of failure.

Liberal critics of the criminal justice system often point to the prisons as a symbol of administrative irrationality. What

17

sense is there, they ask, in a penal policy which far from rehabilitating offenders has a failure rate measured in recidivism often approaching 70 per cent? They miss the point. The prisons do not control the future activities of their inmates: their presence controls the rest of the population. For the threat of being permanently excluded from reasonable work, of social stigmatisation, and of immiseration holds the respectable working class, the honest citizen, constantly in check. This fear is supplemented by an incessant ideological barrage. The mass media are overwhelmingly concerned, whether in news material or in fictional forms, with a discussion of how deviance is an irrationality which is inevitably painful and how conformity produces lasting and substantial rewards.

Nor is such a process of control merely restricted to property offences. Cultures which threaten work discipline, sexual behaviour which undermines the nuclear family, adolescent hedonism are all subject to legal prosecution and distorted coverage in the mass media. Thus when the state of California spends $73 million in 1968 on marihuana control, when more is spent on Social Security prosecutions than has even been obtained illegally from the state, when supposedly scarce police resources are utilized in the persecution of gays, and when legislation denies women the right to choose whether to give birth or not – all this seeming ruling-class irrationality contributes enormously to the maintenance of bourgeois institutions. In short, the persistence of the social order, of the existing class structure and relationships of production, is intimately related to the beliefs and practices surrounding the criminal and the deviant.

Further, the basis for the political support of bourgeois society amongst the mass of the population is closely entwined with their fears of crime and disorder. Just as the ruling class takes real working-class demands for justice and enmeshes them in the support of a class-ridden society, so too, a real need for social order is similarly transmuted. The existence of a class society leads to desperation, demoralisation and a war of all against all. The working-class community suffers immensely from the criminals in its midst. Law gains its support not through a mere mystification of the working class, an ability to render people spellbound by its paraphernalia of pomp and authority.

Legal institutions represent, it is true, the interest of the ruling class but they are also much more than just this. As Herbert Marcuse put it:

> In Marxian theory, the state belongs to the superstructure inasmuch as it is *not* simply the direct political expression of the basic relationships of production but contains elements which, as it were, 'compensate' for the class relationships of production. The state, being and remaining the state of the ruling class, sustains *universal* law and order and thereby guarantees at least a modicum of equality and security for the whole society. Only by virtue of these elements can the class state fulfil the function of 'moderating' and keeping within the bounds of 'order' the class conflicts generated by the production relations. It is this 'mediation' which gives the state the appearance of a universal interest over and above the conflicting particular interests.[7]

The class society which creates social disorganisation also creates its partial palliative. Legal institutions also contain within them gains and concessions wrested from the bourgeoisie by the labour movement; furthermore, they are a repository for the ideals of equality, justice and liberty which, however empty these remain as formal pronouncements outside the economic and political basis necessary to realise them, remain genuine ideals all the same. Conservative law-and-order campaigns therefore play on real needs for social order and embody genuine ideals, albeit in a distorted form. In this fashion, the criminal and the destructive elements of a class society are presented not as *result* of the present society but as the *cause* of its lack of harmony. The ideological impact of such an inversion of the real world is considerable.

5.   The lumpenproletariat

Terms like lumpenproletariat and petty bourgeoisie, used by Marx, lose all meaning if they are torn from their nineteenth-century context and parachuted into the social structure of a specific advanced capitalist society. To deny the Black Power movement with its roots in the structurally unemployed of the ghetto, or the Prison movement with its innumerable heroic examples of collective struggle, any role in the fight for socialism would be short-sighted and doctrinaire in the extreme. This is not – to repeat – to condone the petty theft, arbitrary violence

19

and hustling typical of lumpenproletarian areas. But it is to note the remarkable fashion in which the most downtrodden sections of the population can be transformed by socialist ideas, and to note the enormous violence with which such transformations are met by the ruling class. As George Jackson noted:

> We attempted to transform the black criminal mentality into a black revolutionary mentality. As a result, each of us has been subjected to years of the most vicious reactionary violence by the state. Our mortality rate is almost what you would expect to find in a history of Dachau.[8]

6.   Socialist Society

No one can imagine the disappearance of control in any society but this control can be democratised, it can be informal and it need not involve the near-irrevocable stigmatisation which occurs in present-day capitalist societies and those which Hirst would term 'socialist'. Further, in an advanced socialist society the problems of control would be considerably diminished. For one can imagine a society where the desperation which engenders violent and vicious behaviour is absent, where the war of all against all is supplanted by more fully social forms of community. Thus Lenin writing about the final realisation of communism notes:

> only communism makes the state absolutely unnecessary, for there is *nobody* to be suppressed – 'nobody' in the sense of a *class*, of systematic struggle against a definite section of the population. We are not utopians, and do not in the least deny the possibility and inevitability of excesses on the part of *individual persons* or the need to stop *such* excesses. In the first place, however, no special machine, no special apparatus of suppression, is needed for this; this will be done by the armed people themselves, as simply and readily as any crowd of civilised people, even in modern society, interferes to put a stop to a scuffle, or to prevent a woman from being assaulted. And, secondly, we know that the fundamental social cause of excesses, which consist in the violation of the rules of social intercourse, is the exploitation of the people, their want and their poverty. With the removal of this chief cause, excesses will inevitably *'wither away'*. We do not know how quickly and in what succession, but we do know they will wither away. With their withering away the state will also *wither away*.[9]

Frank Pearce's book is a landmark in the creation of a marxist criminology and a clear rebuttal of those socialists who would view crime as a marginal issue or a diversion from the concerns of marxist theory and practice. It appears at a time when criminologists both in North America[10] and in Europe[11] are taking up explicitly marxist positions. This book will make our collective task easier.

Jock Young
October 1975

Notes

1. George Jackson, *Soledad Brother*, Harmondsworth: Penguin 1971, p.49.
2. H.S.Becker, *Outsiders*, New York: Free Press 1963.
3. D.Matza, *Becoming Deviant*, Englewood Cliffs: Prentice-Hall 1969.
4. P.Q.Hirst, 'Marx and Engels on law, crime and morality', in *Critical Criminology*, (eds.) I.Taylor, P.Walton and J.Young, London: Routledge & Kegan Paul 1975, pp.203–32.
5. *ibid.*, p.240.
6. For a discussion of such a programme see *The Iron Fist and the Velvet Glove*, Berkeley: Center for Research on Criminal Justice 1975, the first publication of the Radical Union of Criminologists.
7. H.Marcuse, *Soviet Marxism*, Harmondsworth: Penguin 1971, p.101.
8. Jackson, *op.cit.*, p.40.
9. V.I.Lenin, *The State and Revolution*, Moscow: Progress Publishers 1969, p.83.
10. The Radical Union of Criminologists who publish the magazine *Crime and Social Justice*, obtainable in this country through the National Deviancy Conference.
11. The European Group for the Study of Deviance and Social Control, c/o Mario Simondi, Dipartimento Statistico, via Curtatone 1, 50123 Firenze, Italy.

1.

Marxism
and Deviancy Theory

1. Labelling Theory and Criminology

Criminology has developed primarily as a policy science; it has been concerned with the practical questions of why people become criminals and what kinds of penal institutions have the best chance of reforming them. This correctional criminology tends to assume both that the criminals who are known to the police and those who are sentenced by the courts are a representative sample of those who commit crimes, and that to engage in criminal behaviour – as opposed to other more acceptable forms of social behaviour – requires some special explanation. These assumptions have been called into question by those writers usually referred to as labelling theorists. They see it as problematic that certain kinds of behaviour are defined as illegal and view the activities of law enforcement agencies, particularly their treatment of the people who come within their influence, as relevant areas of research. For them crime is only a special case of the more general phenomenon of deviance: they are as interested in drug usage, mental illness, homosexuality, prostitution and alcoholism. They argue that definitions of normal, acceptable behaviour and of deviant behaviour vary from society to society and so conformity and deviance are definable only in a relativistic way: there are also many different groups within the same societies who may not agree with each other about what is normal and what is deviant.

In practice social control agencies – the police and courts, the probation service, schools – act as if there is a clear line between the normal and the deviant. They operate using stereotypes of the typical kind of person who will engage in reprehensible behaviour – the work-shy, those from broken homes, the sexually perverted. By using research which has questioned the population as a whole about their activities and which has shown that most people engage at times in socially proscribed behaviour and by studying the interactions that take place between alleged deviants and officials such as the police, it has been shown that those deviants who conform most closely to general stereotypes (the kind of people who have been caught and processed before) are the most likely to end up incarcerated.[1]

The widespread existence of occasional deviance, the under-reporting of crimes, and the filtering out of most rule-breakers as they are processed through the bureaucracies (particularly true of prison populations) means that known deviants cannot be seen as representative of those who commit criminal and/or deviant acts.[2]

The attempt to explain any particular kind of deviant act by examining the characteristics of those who have been processed makes little sense. Howard Becker has pointed out why:

> We can construct workable definitions either of particular actions people might commit or of particular categories of deviance as the world (but not only the authorities) defines them. But we cannot make the two coincide completely, because they do not coincide empirically. They do not coincide empirically because they belong to two distinct, though over-lapping systems of collective action. One consists of the people who co-operate to produce the act in question. The other consists of the people who co-operate in the drama of morality by which 'wrong-doing' is discovered and dealt with, whether that procedure is formal and legal or quite informal.[3]

Whether social scientists attempt to explain crime and deviance in general or some specific example of it such as the use of illegal drugs, they are importing into their explanations the kinds of assumptions made by governmental bureaucracies. As far as they are concerned deviants are the same kind of people because they all equally break the law, whereas the same overt act can be engaged in for many different reasons – marihuana may be used in the same social way as many people use alcohol, it may be a sign of hipness which is a central focus for some people's lives or it may be used for religious purposes.

The labelling theorists argue that the focus of research should shift from looking at individual deviants, with their different reasons for engaging in the activity in question, to investigating the way in which an essentially heterogeneous group of people are pressurised into acting in similar ways by their standardised treatment, by the general stereotypes which inform others' attitudes to them and by the institutional settings in which they find themselves. Such an approach is, as Lemert says:

> . . . a large turn away from older sociology which tended to rest heavily upon the idea that deviance leads to social control. I have come to

believe the reverse idea, i.e. social control leads to deviance, is equally tenable and the potentially richer premise for studying deviance in modern society.[4]

2. Labelling Theory and Symbolic Interactionism

A highly developed and organised human society is one in which the individual members are interrelated in a multiplicity of different intricate and complicated ways, whereby they all share a number of common social interests – interest in, or for the betterment of society – yet on the other hand are more or less in conflict relative to the numerous other interests which they possess only individually or share with one another in small and limited groups.[5]

Labelling theory did not arise in isolation from more general developments in American social thought. It is essentially the application of a particular theory of the relationship between the individual and society to the study of deviance. This theory, known as symbolic interactionism, was developed from the work of George Herbert Mead, a Chicago philosopher interested in social psychology.

Mead in his own work[6] focused on the relationship between individuals and their situation, and the way in which selves developed through social interaction. He was opposing the deterministic view of the individual, which informed much of the psychology current in the early twentieth century. He argued that individuals were not totally determined by their situations but, rather, selected stimuli from the natural and social world.

In other words, he stressed that individuals were not merely passive recipients of the world but through their ability to reflect upon what was happening they could to some extent determine the way in which they, themselves, behaved. In his work he looked at language, socialisation, the development of the conscious mind and of self-identity. His view of society, however, was very underdeveloped and almost summarised by the quotation at the beginning of this section. Later symbolic interactionists have filled out his insights into a more coherent theory and have applied his framework to more concrete social situations.[7]

In the field of deviance it has been developed by many scholars, including Edwin Lemert, Howard Becker, John Kitsuse,

Kai Erikson and Erving Goffman.[8] These writers have applied the theory to many and diverse areas including drug use, sexual expression, mental illness and witchcraft. As indicated above, they have made important contributions to our understanding of the ways in which the social response to such phenomena affects the ways in which those involved will apprehend their experiences and determine the centrality of these experiences for their lives.

3. Edwin Lemert: the Limitations of a Labelling Theorist

Despite the theoretical advances made by these writers they have, in recent years, been subjected to extensive and often effective criticism.[9] Their work promises a great deal but, particularly when confronting the realities of pain, repression and exploitation, signally fails to provide any guidelines to transforming the social world to the more humane place that some of them, at least, present as one of their goals. Rather than repeat these general critiques, I intend to deal in some depth with the thought of one of the most complex of these writers, Edwin Lemert. The detailed development of his thought does vary in certain respects from that of the other members of this school, so that the comments below will not apply equally well to all of them. Nevertheless, such a detailed analysis has many advantages, in particular pinpointing the consistent failure of Lemert adequately to confront historical reality or analyse social structure. After the discussion of Lemert's work I deal with the interactionists in a more general way directing comments to the work of the more radical Howard S. Becker.

Systematic presentations of Lemert's ideas are to be found in his books, *Social Pathology* (1951), *Human Deviance, Social Problems and Social Control* (1967 and 1972), *Social Action and Legal Change: Revolution Within the Juvenile Court* (1970), and innumerable articles including one in *Social Problems*, April 1974, entitled 'Beyond Mead: The Societal Reaction to Deviance'. I have concentrated on the first two books because they provide the clearest expositions of his theoretical views, and, in the case of the earlier work, an analysis of radicalism in America.

As one would expect there are some differences in the formulations to be found in his two main texts due, in part, to positive theoretical development. The former work is strongly influenced by structural-functionalist ideas about the individual and society, whereas the later stresses the plurality of values that can coexist in any one society. But the very real changes in his ideas take place within a set of assumptions that he maintains throughout his work. He retains a belief that a 'theory of deviance' as such can be developed. Lemert says of the earlier book:

> The objective of this work is to study a limited part of deviation, deviation in human behaviour and a certain range of societal reactions, together with their interactional products, and by the methods of science to *arrive at generalisations about the uniformities in these events.* The aim is to study sociopathic behaviour in the same light as normal behaviour and by implication, with extensions or derivations of general sociological theory. (emphasis added)[10]

In the later work he reaffirms this commitment:

> The sociology of deviance must be a science of deviance, and must remain an integral part of a science of social control broadly conceived to discover things necessary to do as well as those not to do.[11]

In *Social Pathology* he defines his task as the application of 'middle range theory' to the field of deviance.[12] He outlines his theory in the following terms:

> 1. There are modalities in human behavior and clusters of deviations from these modalities which can be identified and described for situations specified in time and space.
> 2. Behavioural deviations are a function of culture conflict which is expressed through social organisation.
> 3. There are societal reactions to deviations ranging from strong approval through indifference to strong disapproval.
> 4. Sociopathic behavior is deviation which is *effectively* disapproved.
> 5. The deviant person is one whose role, status, function, and self-definition are importantly shaped by how much deviation he engages in, by the degree of its social visibility, by the particular exposure he has to the societal reaction, and by the nature and strength of the societal reaction.
> 6. There are patterns of restriction and freedom in the social participation of deviants which are related directly to their status, role and self definitions. The biological strictures upon social participation of deviants are directly significant in comparatively few cases.
> 7. Deviants are individualised with respect to their vulnerability to the

societal reaction because: (a) the person is a dynamic agent, (b) there is a structuring to each personality which acts as a set of limits within which the societal reaction operates.[13]

This theory is embedded within more general assumptions about the nature of American society. These are derived from structural-functionalist theory and include the following, which can be drawn out of Lemert's writings:

a. American society is a system held together by a consensus of norms and values. Quite what these are is unclear and is often only discovered in the breach; however 'normal' Americans are conformist most of the time.
b. Normally the system is adequately integrated but on occasion it is disturbed; when this occurs some unspecified self-correcting mechanism leads it to resume its previous stability.
c. Whilst occasional deviance is widespread it is usually caused by situational pressures (which pass with the specific situation) pushing people away from normal conformist behavior.
d. The source of such situational pressures is culture conflict and this refers to situations which bring incompatible social or group pressures to bear upon persons in such a way as to generate unintegrated tensions or anxieties which are expressed in aberrant or novel behavior.[4]

There is little point in providing here a critique of structural functionalism, as this has been done effectively elsewhere. Instead of repeating this, I will concentrate on Lemert's account of radicalism, which shows clearly the limitations imposed by his frame of reference – his lack of 'value freedom' and his lack of scientificity; he bypasses the struggle of ideas and class forces that ultimately determined the drift of American history.

4. Radicalism

Radicalism generally has been held to be the advocacy of ideas and beliefs at variance with those of the majority of the group, community or society. It consists of deviations in the overt, verbal-symbolic behavior of individuals and groups.[15]

Who become radicals? Why? How important are they? What effect does the societal response have on them? What determines the nature of this response? These are the questions that Lemert tries to answer. He writes that:

A cross-sectional role analysis of the radicals in a given society will reveal not only a number of symbolically disordered persons but also

> a large number, perhaps the majority, of persons who profess the extremist beliefs because of general or specific situational pressures.[16]

He cites as an example the pattern of recruitment to the Communist Party:

> During the 1930s in the United States, particularly after 1934, large numbers of middle class professional persons, artists, students and other 'intellectuals' turned towards communism either as 'fellow travellers' or as actual communist party members . . . The trend may be explained by reference to the shattering blow dealt our society by the economic depression of the time, the ideological poverty of indigenous American radicalism, and the slowness of the traditional political parties to appreciate the mounting threat of a European war. The situational nature of the allegiance to the communist programme stood out in sharp relief with the whole-sale desertion of the communist cause by 'fellow travellers' when the pact between Russia and Nazi Germany was announced.[17]

Radicals are seen as being outside society, people whose aims and structural positions are not located within the normal stream of everyday life.

> In the estimation of non-radicals with whom the radical participant comes into contact, he is either a worthless or dangerous member of society . . . In terms of the middle class values of our society, values stressing occupational stability, working towards advancement, and family responsibility he is a failure; his behavior is misguided and his life mis-spent.[18]

Such structurally marginal people cannot influence others through any rational methods but only through propaganda, manipulation, infiltration, distortion, etc. The presupposition of their marginality and the stress on their dubious methods is made very evident when Lemert writes of the 'labor unions in which radicals have infiltrated'.[19] Their ideas are seen as un-American, essentially alien to the indigenous traditions.[20] Lemert asserts that radicalism has failed to spread in America because of its unsuitability as a way of understanding the world and as a guide to political action. Practical experience of failure forces the more sensible of its adherents to revise their views;[21] and the only mature course is to recognise that.

> The real power of American radical organisations, where it has existed, undeniably has come from federations, and affiliating and co-operating groups. In other words, where radical groups have realistically adapted their organisation to the fractionalised power distributions in our society and worked informally to achieve their aims, they have been most successful.[33]

31

Most of the educated people who dabble with such fanciful ideas eventually mature and

> . . . accept the conventional philosophical or theological resolutions of their conflict. Failing this, many become more comfortable with their conflicts compromising their ideas by contenting themselves with the more generalised satisfactions of family life, the knowledge of a job well done even though its importance may be quite small. Still others seek outlets in forms of sociopathic behavior such as drinking, gambling, carousing or compulsive indulgence in hobbies and sports.[23]

By definition then radicalism will never achieve its goals in American society. It has no hope of influencing the electorate, or of persuading the mass of people to overthrow the social system. Nevertheless, there may be a need for the society to take certain kinds of precautions against radicals, since they are un-American and manipulative.

> A society in which nationalism is one of the integrating norms will of necessity make sure that overt sabotage and treasonable behavior will be kept at a minimum in administrative agencies carrying the burden of national defense or offense. It will also eliminate untrustworthy workers from those parts of its technological organisation directly related to waging of war. Clear cut cases of sabotage, conspiracy and treason can be detected and prosecuted, but the borderline cases pose special problems. Punitive forces against workers in government or industry for written or spoken utterances which sounded as if 'they might' act contrary to national interest or for mere membership in organisations in which there are, or have been, known espionage agents can be tremendously damaging to the morale of such workers.[24]

Yet, as Lemert acknowledges, the response to radicalism has often gone much further than this involving a great deal of punitive action against radicals this century. This requires some explanation since, being alien and marginal, they must, almost by definition, be impotent. McCarthyism needs explaining if there is already adequate protection for society in the common law and the law of treason.[25]

The irrational social response is understood by Lemert as a product of the interaction between inaccurate stereotypes, sustained by generalised prejudices, the general illegality of police behaviour in the USA, the operations of the particular interests backing anti-radical groups and the nature of the radicals' own provocative behaviour.[26] He sees no particular bias because there is often good cause for police anger.

The drive of revolutionaries to weaken or overthrow established power, and the need of other radical groups to advance their causes through parades and public meetings, bring them almost always into conflict with the police. This conflict was particularly great at one time between anarchists and the police as a consequence of the formers' deliberate philosophy of the propaganda crime. Communists, too, have deliberately sought to provoke the police into breaking up their parades and meetings as a means of obtaining evidence of the 'police persecution of the working class'.[27]

Lemert's overall assessment of the potential of radicalism, and the reasons for the somewhat extreme reaction of the social control agencies to its presence is as follows:

The specious character of the societal reaction to radicalism has been especially obtrusive in the history of American culture. A number of writers have pertinently commented upon the hysteria of fear which sweeps over our populace from time to time, a fear of things alien, insidious and subversive. The years immediately succeeding the two world wars were noteworthy in this country for extravaganzas of counter-espionage and press campaigns of vilification and harassment directed at radicals and their organisations. The basic irrationality of the social reaction of these times was attested to by the radicals themselves who asked rhetorically: 'why do they fear us so much when we are so few?' . . . Operational demonstrations of the thin substance composing the societal reaction are seen in the administrative clemency leading to reduction and commutation of sentences of imprisoned radicals after the crisis has vanished and the society slowly resumes its previous stability.[28]

Lemert presupposes that the radical view is one which cannot provide a meaningful solution to anybody's problems in American society. He does not come to this conclusion by confronting radicals' arguments, their analysis of capitalism, and by so doing demonstrating their intellectual and practical poverty; he merely asserts the contrary as being self-evident. But what warrant is there for such intellectual 'imperialism'? Paul Walton makes this point well when he asks:

How can we, then, apply deviancy theory to the understanding of a deviant group whose perspectives and reflexivity are often as developed and, in some cases, superior to, the framework which is intended to explain them?[29]

It is arrogant to believe that some allegedly scientific sociological theory is necessarily superior to the understanding developed by the people who are actually in the situation being analysed. This superiority has to be demonstrated; it cannot be assumed *a priori*.

Not only does Lemert not confront the arguments of radicals but his empirical discussion of radicalism is empiricist at its best and factually inaccurate at its worst. In his descriptions he merely lists the different kinds of people who have been radicals at particular times but fails to put their beliefs in context by relating them to the changing socio-economic conditions under which radicals have lived. For example, he writes:

> In 1912 the greater strength of the American socialist party seemed to lie in smaller towns, and the states where its candidates received the heaviest votes were primarily agricultural states: Kansas, Minnesota, Oklahoma, Nevada, Montana, Arizona, Washington, California and Idaho.'[30]

He does not connect the appeal of socialism in agricultural areas to the monopolisation of agriculture occurring at that time or to the fact that capitalistic organisation of agriculture produced wage labourers. He merely concludes from this discussion that:

> While it can be shown that rural people often have participated in radical movements, it remains debateable whether, in a sociological sense, rural radicals are differentiated in ways comparable to urban radicals.[31]

He assumes that categories such as rural/urban distinguish scientifically between different forms of life – he ignores the question of whether 'rural' describes a slave, feudal, peasant, independent producer or capitalist form of agriculture.

He is, furthermore, often factually wrong. In his treatment of the relationship that women have to the movement he asserts that 'many wives and sweethearts of radicals undoubtedly reflect their views or follow them into a revolutionary organisation simply to be near them and share their lives'.[32] As a necessary consequence of this view he concludes: 'Most women who have entered into radical groups have probably done so for reasons other than deep sincere identification with the group objectives.'[33] This is nonsense: militant feminists for instance, were an essential part of the socialist movement.[34]

Indeed his whole account of the history of socialism is distorted. Although the American ruling class successfully pre-empted the development of a large social-democratic party, there

34

was – until the late 1940s – a real *socialist potential* in America. The socialist parties were strong until the 1920s and during this period the revolutionary Industrial Workers of the World was a significant voice in the trade-union movement; in the 1930s communist and social-democratic trade unionists were involved in the leftist Congress of Industrial Organisations (itself not as radical as much rank-and-file activity); and in the 1940s there was still a real socialist presence in the unions.[35]

The failure of socialism to achieve effective parliamentary expression was due, in part at least, to the strategies of the American ruling class; they were only too aware of the possibilities for socialism. Naked violence has always been used against trade unionists, but during the 1930s when working-class self-consciousness was increasing this was linked with attempts to support and incorporate the more reactionary trade unionists. Lemert admits that illegal methods of repression have been used against working class organisers.

> It has been brought out that the sheriff departments in some areas have literally worked under orders of corporate agriculture, mining and lumbering interests, invoking the power of their offices to break strikes and incidentally deny rights of free speech, assembly, and a swift trial to labor organisers and radicals alike.[36]

He treats these activities and their direction by corporate interests as a 'fact of life' – in the same way as he casually mentions that anti-radical organisations 'possess little real appeal to the broad public, receiving their support almost entirely from corporate business and industrial interests'.[37]

Yet he does not recognise the partiality of the state towards the interests of capital. However, as Kolko, Weinstein, Woodiwiss and others have argued, between the 1890s and the 1920s it was brought firmly under the control of corporate capital.[38]

When the ruling class's control of the state is linked with its recognition that there is no necessary unanimity of interest within society and of the spread of a commitment to socialism, then the societal 'over response' can be seen to have exhibited hidden rationality.

In other words, there are circumstances where, if left unrepressed, *socialist ideas will spread because of their relevance*, not simply because of deception, manipulation or propaganda.

35

This explains why the 'societal reaction' has often been so strong and in many cases even illegal, where to stay within the bounds of the American constitution might have allowed for the spread of socialist ideas.

The suppression of the freedom of speech and the right to organise is necessary in order to maintain the stability of the system. The persecution of socialists, particularly Wobblies, during the First World War and the use of illegal techniques, smear campaigns and misrepresentation are all well documented, as is the use made of gangsters during the 1930s and 1940s to smash socialist organisation in the trade unions.

Overreactions will be tolerated where they have such a hidden rationality but will be eliminated when they are no longer useful.

This was certainly true of McCarthyism. The public declarations by the British and American governments soon after the close of the Second World War that there existed a 'cold war' were not immediately received with great enthusiasm in either of the two countries. During the mid-1940s the dominant capitalist powers became very aware of widespread international sympathy for socialist ideas; this was so in much of Europe, in Britain and inside America itself.

One of the functions of the cold war myths generated by the Western Allies after the Second World War was to achieve stability and to maintain the international empires, if necessary by force of arms. In the immediate post war years:

> Because of the wartime role of the Soviet Union (and the pro-Soviet pro-Stalin propaganda that had been spread, not without a large element of Czarism, by Western governments in a western press), plus the relative freedom which Stalin in fact permitted in Eastern Europe in 1945 and the restraint he imposed on the communist parties of western Europe it was not possible to secure public support for an immediate showdown with Russia.[39]

McCarthyism and Truman's cold war policies helped make the American public accept intervention in world affairs. They also managed to limit the spread of radicalism within the USA itself. That McCarthyism was only tolerated as long as it was useful to the American ruling class can be seen by the way that McCarthy lost his power when he overstepped the limit

36

of his 'brief'. (That is not to say that he was actually given one, but that he was only tolerated when he was acting in the general interest of the American ruling class.)

> The Business Advisory Council may have triggered the squelch of McCarthy that had been smouldering in many upper class minds. The incident was his high-handed treatment of yet another member of the power elite, corporate leader Robert T.Stevens, of Andover, Yale, J.P.Stevens and Company, General Electric and Morgan Guarantee Trust. He was serving as the Secretary of the Army when he was embarrassed by the McCarthy on nation-wide television. During the May 1954 meeting at Homestead, Stevens flew down from Washington for a weekend reprieve from his televised torture. A special delegation of BAC officials made it a point to journey from the hotel to the mountaintop airport to greet Stevens. He was escorted through the lobby like a conquering hero. Then, publicly, one member of the BAC after another roasted the Eisenhower administration for its McCarthy appeasement policy. The BAC's attitude gave the administration some courage as shortly thereafter former Senator Ralph Flanders (a Republican BAC member) introduced a Senate resolution calling for censure.[40]

Soon after, McCarthy fell from power. Even if the internal communist threat seemed real to J. Edgar Hoover, the head of the FBI, his hysterical propaganda mystified the nature of radicalism and led people to believe that the problem was one of a foreign origin rather than something which related to an indigenous American tradition. It seems unlikely, however, that the more sophisticated members of the American ruling class shared his analysis of radicalism in the national and international context. Hoover claimed, in 1965, that:

> ... Communism is a vast international conspiracy which today dominates one third of the earth's people. Here in our own country, that conspiracy is represented by the Communist Party, USA, a bold and defiant band of anti-American turncoats whose operations are directed and controlled by the Kremlin in Moscow... Yet in country after country, there still remain the legions of uninformed, misinformed, and politically naive who are the non-Communist dupes and fellow travellers... We find these dupes in shocking abundance in our own United States where Gus Hall, the Moscow trained General Secretary of the Communist Party USA, boasted to newsmen last fall that there are approximately 100,000 Americans within the Party's influence. About 10 per cent of them he said, are dues paying members. The remainder he described as close sympathisers.[41]

Although Hoover's assessment of the significance of the Communist Party in the radical movement in America was inaccurate, he had the *power* to enforce his interpretations – to act as if his assessment of reality was correct. He was able to imprison, harass and intimidate people, to stop the spread of socialism by a mixture of repression and misrepresentation. His ideological understanding of the world was a partial rationality, but one which seemed a total rationality because of the power he had at his disposal. The seemingly irrational overreaction of social control agencies, then, can be seen to function for the interests of the ruling groups in American society.

Thus an analysis of McCarthyism shows that Lemert's account of the dynamics determining the actions of social control agencies is both inadequate and inaccurate.

5. From Consensualism to Pluralism

With the decline of rabid anti-communism, the 'cold war' influences on Lemert's thought waned. His later work has stressed the pluralistic nature of modern, complex industrial societies. He places more emphasis on the diversity of values in society and questions the assumption of general social homogeneity.

In both *Social Pathology* and *Human Deviance, Social Problems and Social Control*, he suggests that not only is deviance very common in that any individual may commit such acts but that there is a tremendous diversity of values inside the society. This view remains a qualified one, however, for in his distinction between passive and active social control, Lemert still suggests that there is a basic consensus of values inside the society:

> The distinction, a pivotal one for our purposes, makes passive control an aspect of conformity to traditional norms; active social control on the other hand is a process for the implementation of goals and values. The former has to do with the maintenance of social order, the latter with emergent social integrations.[42]

He spells out this distinction in more detail earlier in the same chapter:

> Thus, in addition to the older body of criminal laws revolving around sacred values of life, person and property, there is a vast proliferation of criminal statutes having to do with health, welfare, public safety and order, conservation, taxes, banking, fiduciary operations, insurance

38

and transportation, largely representing the specialised values of associations. In many instances the legal norms represent no values of individuals or groups, but rather are the results of compromises reached through group interaction in legislatures.[43]

This formulation is quite compatible with pluralism, and indeed Lemert characterises his perspective as 'neo-technic pluralism'. By this he means that while there is a basic consensus in society about the way to resolve disagreements and reach agreement for a large number of groups with their own goals and values, the direction of social change is not simply the chance outcome of the interactions between these groups but is determined by the exigencies of technology.[44] This stress on technology allows Lemert to explain social order and social change without falling foul of the dangers of pure subjectivism, of treating society as independent of the material world.[45] Criticising Sutherland's analysis of white-collar crime, he argues that:

> The behavior and verbal rationales of corporation executives which so incensed Sutherland – such as their willingness to put profits above patriotism – from our point of view can be understood in the context of the technological and cost imperatives that confront whole associations.[46]

> Data of my own indicate that fines for violations of weight regulation for trucks in areas of northern California are accepted by companies, as well as by individual truck drivers, as necessary cost of doing business. Compliance or non-compliance becomes a matter of dollars and cents.[47]

The second quotation makes clear that the crucial factor is not technology as such, but rather technology utilised within the social relationships defined by capitalism. Although he does not integrate it into his analysis Lemert does recognise at times that technology is not simply an abstraction: 'There seems to be evidence of a growth of 'practical morality' under the influence of the dominant world of business, industry and the large associations.'[48] Overall Lemert never really confronts the role of capitalism within his society: he does not recognise that, as Karsten Struhl put it, 'The men at the top must heed the basic law of American society, the need to expand corporate profit.'[49]

6. The Pervasiveness of Pluralism

Lemert, as he himself has indicated, is a pluralist. It is

a commitment that he shares with most of those who use labelling theory. Stuart Hills, for example, argues that:

> In a rapidly changing pluralistic society such as the United States . . . with its racial, religious, ethnic and class diversity; its sharply competing economic and political interest groups; its conflicting lifestyles and value orientations among different sub-cultures; and its frequent recourse to the criminal law to regulate and prohibit a wide variety of behavior – the *interest group* perspective would seem more useful in understanding the enactment and selective enforcement of laws involving marihuana, drug use, organised crime, and white collar crime . . . each of these three crime areas involves considerable public ambivalence, an absence of widespread consensus, conflicting moral codes and interests, and activity by strong and powerful interest groups to influence legislation and its application.[50]

It is worth spending some time elaborating and criticising this way of interpreting the operation of the political processes within American society. To do so it is necessary to spell out the mainstream view – that which informs Lemert's work – the criticisms of it from within American political science which have developed what Tony Woodiwiss has characterised as 'radical pluralism' – a view shared by some of the labelling theorists such as Howard Becker – and then to criticise them all from a marxist viewpoint.

Pluralism is a theory of politics and tries to answer the questions: who rules and for whom? It sees:

> American society as fractured into congeries of hundreds of small special interest groups with incompletely overlapping memberships widely different power bases and a multitude of techniques for exercising influence and decisions salient to them . . .[51]

More systematically, pluralists believe that:

1. There are no power elites; power is widely distributed in the communities;
2. Power is always directly applied and observable;
3. Community power should be investigated with case studies of 'important decisions';
4. Only decisions made by formal political bodies or persons should be studied; and
5. The power system is 'slack' in allowing for social change within it.[52]

Studies informed by this view have been undertaken at both the national and local level. Edwin Lemert's study of the changes in the juvenile court system in California is in this vein.[53]

The major index for measuring power used by pluralists is the question: who influences 'important decisions'? However, there is nothing in their framework which allows one to differentiate between 'important' and other kinds of decisions. Furthermore, there is no recognition that many of the most important issues in a society may never become decisions since the possibility of raising them is precluded in advance.

> All forms of political organisation have a bias in favor of the exploitation of some kinds of conflict and the suppression of others, because organisation is the mobilisation of bias. Some issues are organised into politics while others are organised out.[54]

Such considerations entail the introduction of an historical dimension into the discussion and a recognition of the unrealised possibilities in the situations being analysed. A specification of the fundamental structural arrangements inside the society provides criteria for evaluating both what important decisions are made and those that are not even discussed. More concretely, in the American context, the effective consolidation by corporate capital over the national and local political processes precludes raising issues within a framework that takes its interests for granted.

Trenchant criticism has thus been made of the pluralists' analysis of local politics. Todd Gittlin has shown that a re-examination of Dahl's data on New Haven and Banfield's on Chicago[55] demonstrates that, contrary to their conclusions, major decisions in those cities have always been made in such a way that the corporate rich are not threatened.[56] This critique is in a 'radical pluralist' vein,[57] the perspective that informs the work of writers such as Bachrach and Baratz, and much of the output of Howard Becker as well as of Irving Louis Horowitz and Edwin Sutherland.

Radical pluralists share with their conservative counterparts a belief that society is made up of a plurality of different groups with different interests; they differ, however, in their recognition that not all such groups benefit from the workings of the system. The lack of effective power in the hands of the poor, blacks, drug users, women, youth and homosexuals, means that they are always the losers in the competitive social world: the rules under which they live are not theirs. Howard Becker puts it in the following terms:

> Differences in the ability to make rules and apply them to other people are essentially power differentials (either legal or extra-legal). Those groups whose social position gives them weapons and power are best able to enforce their rules. Distinctions of age, sex, ethnicity, and class are all related to differences in power, which accounts for differences in the degree to which groups so distinguished can make rules for others.[58]

The sociologist having recognised this must also recognise that more powerful individuals will not only attempt to impose their values on the other people in society generally, but also on those who study social life.[59] Hence a recognition that society works in an irrational and unjust manner calls into question the taken-for-granted picture of the world and is therefore inherently political.

The recognition that deviants are unjustly treated, are playing a system rigged against them, leads Becker and his colleagues to demand 'fairness'. They see their role as one of demystifying the stereotypes of deviants. They point out the ironic and expensive consequences of stigmatising deviants (e.g. drug addicts may be pushed by the demands of their expensive illegal habit to mugging), and try to persuade the public and administrators that too much interference in everyday life leads to more trouble than it is worth. They argue that, despite the opposition that he might experience, the deviance theorist should articulate the 'reality' of the deviant's world and the ways in which it is moulded by contact with official agencies. It may be necessary for the deviants to organise politically in order to be heard; but when they are heard then a social contract can be made whereby the mores of diversity will be respected by all groups. Becker in his comments on the campus drug problem suggests it would be solved if the campus authorities ignored it to avoid public scandal *and*, in exchange for this, students played it cool.[60] Another example is the suggestion that the success or otherwise of anti-poverty programmes is dependent upon the degree to which the poor themselves participate in their operation. The reasoning behind this is that such participation encourages the development of a sense of self-interest amongst those groups that do not already possess it.[61]

Their solution to social disadvantage and to oppression is to remove stereotypes and organise the deviants so that they can effectively participate in American society and the political system so that it is working properly. Bachrach and Baratz express their confidence when they write: 'This kind of system as the American experience bears witness, can serve well the interests of most of the citizenry.'[62] The evasion about the relevant criteria for judging its effectiveness and their failure to provide evidence for such an optimistic assessment are clear. Above all they also lack an effective historical dimension and thus:

> Their analyses will continue to suffer through remaining locked within the rather narrow confines of the liberal problematic, which is forever asking them to 'reconcile irreconcilables', i.e. how to achieve social justice without undermining the foundation stone of bourgeois society, the right to private property.[63]

It is the needs of the corporate rich in America, the top one per cent of spending units who own more than 75 per cent of marketable stock, that are first catered for by the American political system. For despite 'progressive taxation', increased welfare benefits and state education, there has been no substantial redistribution of wealth; corporate interests control both the Republican and the Democratic Party; organisations representing large-scale business are most influential in both domestic and foreign policy. And, as I will show later, the New Deal itself was a part of the process by which monopoly capitalism achieved hegemonic domination over American society. There was never any doubt of Roosevelt's commitment to capitalism, but in order to save it from itself he was forced to give it some rather unpalatable medicine.

The strategies used by the capitalist class in their struggle against the development of a socialist consciousness amongst the working class have been clearly documented by Edward Hayes in his book *Power Structure and Urban Policy: Who Rules in Oakland?* He shows how business and professional groups used political manipulation, the media and, in illegal ways, the police, to maintain their hegemonic domination, both nationally and locally.

In Oakland although these groups exerted a highly visible political influence from the beginning of the century, corporate growth and a desire to encourage it even further by lowering taxes, together with a desire to undermine the power of the Socialist Party amongst the working class, led to proposals for charter reform, i.e. for changes in the mode of city government. The Oakland socialists who had polled 9,837 votes in 1911 were only narrowly defeated by the property party with 11,732 votes. To head off the danger posed by a party which demanded nationalisation of the corporations, the city's business and professional groups convened a meeting of freeholders who were almost exclusively drawn from their own ranks. They decided to change to a commission form of government so that, instead of having both a city council and separate directors for fire, public works, and other city departments, city commissioners would combine the roles of councilmen (legislators) and department directors (executives). The practical result was that, on the one hand, monies saved by such 'streamlining' were used to promote local business interests and, on the other, the introduction of the 'non-partisan' ballot which forbade the use of party labels helped to decimate the socialist vote in 1913.

After a period of relative quiescence the next upsurge of working-class activity was again treated as a threat:

> The business community was completely united during the 1930s in opposing unionisation of public and private employees, in the growth of the CIO. It united vocally, publicly and unequivocally to denounce the general strike in 1947 and to press its viewpoint on the city government.[64]

This strike was the last coordinated expression of working-class power to date.

It is not surprising that Hayes summarises his findings as follows:

> [Thus] across the wide range of public policies in the protection of their basic interests, the city's medium and large businessmen have reaped the major and continuing benefits of local policy, while the non-rich have reaped the harvest of more crowded housing, forced removal, relatively higher taxes, and minimum public services. Such organisations as Unions and Neighborhood Groups have influenced the policy processes to some extent as pressure groups but so far been unable to influence the election of major city or county officials or to bring about the redirection of

public monies or broad based effort to solve the problems of the poor or working classes. To call this a government of all the people would be a fiction.

It would be more descriptive to speak of the city's political system as operating in the context of an economic system which has preponderant influence over public policies and which allows scope only to those public solutions which do not encroach on the interests of the private economy . . . This system of power and policy formation has led to protest, rebellion, and militant organisation by those whose interests have not been elevated to the level of policy – unorganised labor as long as 30 years ago and non-whites today.[65]

Later in this essay I will spell out an alternative marxist way of analysing American society but first I wish to make some further comments on labelling theory.

7. Empiricism and Interactionism

In his article, 'Labelling Theory Reconsidered', Howard Becker, in answering criticisms made by radicals, asserted the possibility of establishing 'a continuity between the analysis of society-wide class groupings characteristic of [the Marxist] tradition and the more intensive study of smaller units characteristic of interactionist theories of deviance'.[66] Clearly he misunderstands marxism and its starting point, the specification of the mode of production. This is composed of the social classes organised in relations of production to utilise the forces of production. The distinction between a class-in-itself and a class-for-itself involves a programmatic recognition that the subcultural social organisation of people in everyday life does not necessarily follow objective class lines and this is particularly true for the working class. A major aim of political action is to assist the proletariat to identify itself as a class over and above whatever ethnic, religious or geographical identifications already exist. Thus one does not automatically start from the already present group identifications. To do so is a form of empiricism, a central characteristic of symbolic interactionism. Whether they accept the judgements of the powerful or give a sympathetic ear to the complaints of the oppressed, deviancy theories allow their field of study to be circumscribed by the givenness of social definitions.

45

If there are no frictions, no articulated complaints, then there seems to be nothing to study. The roots of this view, as well as of its pluralist foundations, can be found in the work of George Herbert Mead. For him and many other intellectuals in his era, society and science were transformed into the bureaucratic image:

> Instead of likening society to a clock's simple gears in perpetual motion, men were thinking in terms of a complex social technology, of a mechanised and systematised factory. Science, the basic word that every school of thought claimed and worshipped, also altered in meaning to accommodate the revolution...Science had become a procedure, or an orientation, rather than a body of results. When it still did connote exact truths, it referred to something very specific – the doctor's microbe – not to the laws of a world order.[67]

The links between these formulations and social thought can be seen in Mead's discussion of 'The Working Hypothesis in Social Reform'.

> The highest criterion that we can present is that the hypothesis shall work in the complex of forces into which we introduce it. We can never set up a detailed statement of the conditions that are to be ultimately attained. What we have is a method and a control and application, not an ideal to work toward...In social reform, or the application of intelligence to the control of social conditions, we must make a like assumption and this assumption takes the form of belief in the essentially social character of the human impulse and endeavour.[68]

The implications of these images of science and society can be seen in Mead's substantive work. He was interested in the possibilities of the elimination of crime, the development of an 'effective and just' juvenile court system and the development of a relevant educational system. However, as Tony Platt has shown, the substantive meaning of such interests was linked with the interests of corporate capital. The development of special laws and courts for juveniles,

> The child saving movement tried to do for the criminal justice system what industrialists and corporate leaders were trying to do for the economy . . . That is, achieve order, stability and control while preserving the existing class system and distribution of wealth. While the child saving movement, like most progressive reforms, had its most active and visible supporters in the middle class and professions, it would not have been capable of achieving significant reforms without the financial and political support of the wealthy and powerful.[69]

Not surprisingly then, when Mead analyses crime he comes

to the same conclusion as Durkheim – that crime, or at least its punishment, is necessary for society in that it helps define group norms and boundaries.

There are two untenable assumptions in such analyses: that there are shared interests and that there is a unitary set of values or 'collective representations'. As opposed to this view, I would argue that in capitalist societies some collective representations are used to induce false consciousness in the working class. Historically it is clear that there are usually rival criteria for identifying in-groups and out-groups, particularly international class identifications as opposed to nationalistic identifications with individual capitalist states.[70]

Mead's recognition that stigmatising the deviant has ironic consequences still takes as the scientific problem that of the administrators. Thus he writes:

> Hostility towards the lawbreaker inevitably brings with it the attitudes of retribution, repression and exclusion. These provide no principles for the eradication of crime, for returning the delinquent to normal social relations, nor for stating the transgressed rights and institutions in terms of their positive social functions.[71]

If a particular field of study is being developed, then some criteria must be used to determine what should be included and what excluded. In theory, at least, all kinds of deviance (including upper-class crimes, and the possession of rare but valued characteristics) could be studied; in the event they rarely are. But more importantly these theorists only investigate the occasions when deviance is alleged by some inter-actant in the situation. As a result, they rarely look at the actions of the powerful.

> Because of these biases, there is an implicit, but very clear, acceptance by these authors of the current definitions of 'deviance'. It comes about because they concentrate their attention on those who have been successfully labeled 'deviant', and not on those who break laws, fix laws, violate ethical and moral standards, harm individuals and groups, etc., but who either are able to hide their actions, or when known can deflect criticism, labeling, and punishment.[72]

In other words, the problems looked at are those faced by the ruling class in making their social system work well. Lemert, for instance, in *Social Pathology* deals with those who are not active and useful members of American society, those who are rendered unproductive by blindness, speech defects, radicalism, crime, drunkenness, mental disorders, or involvement in prostitution.

Gouldner recognises this and accuses such an approach of seeing the underdog:

> as someone who has to be managed, and should be managed better, by a bureaucratic apparatus of official caretakers. In short, it conceives of the underdog as someone maltreated by a bureaucratic establishment whose remedial efforts are brutal, and whose rule enforcement techniques are self-interested. While it sees deviance as generated by a process of social interaction, as emerging out of the *matrix of an unanalysed society*, *it does not see deviance as deriving from specified master institutions of this larger society*, or as expressing an active opposition to them. [emphasis added][73]

Thus whilst Lemert identifies with ruling class interests, Becker can at best be a somewhat righteous and reactive critic. Marxism, on the other hand, can help in the transformation of these repressive societies.

8.   The State in Bourgeois Thought

There is very little discussion of the state in most sociological accounts of crime and deviance. An exception is found in the work of David Matza, a sympathiser with labelling theory, whose *Becoming Deviant*, communicates a real sense of the state's overwhelming power. He tries to develop a dialectical account of the interaction between conscious subjects and massive unyielding institutions by mobilising a whole set of descriptive concepts: 'ban', 'being bedevilled', 'transparency', 'apprehension', 'being cast', 'exclusion', 'the display of authority', 'the building of identity', and 'collective representation'. He also shows that the state's importance lies as much in the fear of being disobedient which it invokes among the respectable, as in the transformation of the lives and consciousness of those apprehended by it.

Whilst this is an advance on most work on crime and deviance, Matza's discussion is so abstract and ahistorical as to provide little guidance to understanding the operation of the state in a particular society at some given historical moment. This would require a specification of the importance accorded to the state by the dominant legitimating ideology within that society. It would depend on the actual institutions making it up and their interrelations; on the role of that ideology in integrating and coordinating the society; on its role within the economy; how responsible it is for controlling the everyday activities of its subjects; on the degree of power and influence of those confronting it and on the amount of partiality it shows. Matza's analysis lacks any 'political economy'. His subjectivist methodology, by taking as its *starting* point individual social meanings, produces as its natural counterpart an abstract structuralism which provides as the overall basis of social order the entity of Leviathan: social institutions other than individual and state are only introduced in an ad hoc manner.

For Matza uses the same term for the state as Thomas Hobbes, sharing a central concern with the relationship between the powerful state and the atomised individuals making up society. He differs from Hobbes in his recognition that the war of all against all is more likely to be one between different groups than between individuals; i.e. he is a pluralist. Matza, Becker and other labelling theorists think it wrong to legally prohibit drug use, sexual diversity, juvenile non-conformity or bizarre behaviour. They see state interference with these aspects of everyday life as unwarranted since these are often 'crimes without victims'[74] or relatively trivial. This view seems far from Hobbes, yet the distance is not so much between the basic categories as between the realities being investigated.

For Hobbes the state was needed for the reproduction of social life – to guarantee individuals, control over their own means of subsistence. The seventeenth century was an age of scarcity, when long hours of work were necessary to feed, clothe and shelter the population as a whole and work dominated all aspects of existence. In contemporary America leisure has become more and more important both in quantity and in its centrality for people's lives, and the bulk of the output of the labelling theorists has been concerned with leisure activities; in this area they see Leviathan as having no legitimate function. They do not refute Hobbes's pessimism but rather avoid the issues faced by Hobbes since they take for granted the reproduction of social life. They ignore society's dependence on a functioning economy and do not see the essential role played by the authoritarianism of Leviathan (and authoritarianism within industry) in maintaining what is, after all, a capitalist organisation of production and distribution. They forget that:

> The first presupposition of all human existence, and therefore of all history,... is that...men must be in a position to live in order to be able to 'make history'. But life involves everything else – eating and drinking, a habitation, clothing, and many other things. The first historical act is, therefore, the production of material life itself. This is indeed a historical act, a fundamental condition of all history, which today, as thousands of years ago, must be accomplished every day and every hour merely in order to sustain human life.[75]

There is a two-fold implication for the analysis of the state and society. First, that any adequate theorising requires a scientific analysis of the society as a whole; secondly, that the importance of the state within this overall structure must be specified.

Agents of the ruling class such as lawyers and politicians often have a very clear idea of the relationship between the state and the society as a whole. In Britain the Franks Committee stated in 1972 that:

> A safe and independent life for a nation and its people requires effective defence against the threat of attack from outside. It requires the maintenance of the nation's relations with the rest of the world, and of its essential economic base. It requires the preservation of law and order, and the ability to cope with emergencies threatening the essential services. The country's constitutional arrangements should be capable of fulfilling these requirements.[76]

The outcry about the dangers of anarchy often links together actions like crimes of personal violence, property offences, strikes and political demonstrations and the last two are often condemned for violating the 'rule of law'.

This doctrine is an important one in Anglo-American law. The 1962 Royal Commission on the Police claimed that British liberty:

> . . . depends on the supremacy of Parliament and on the rule of law. We do not accept that the criterion of a police state is whether a country's police force is national rather than local...The proper criterion is whether the police are answerable to the law and, ultimately, to a democratically elected Parliament . . .

> The police in this country are the instrument for enforcing the rule

of law; they are the means by which civilised society maintains order that people may live safely in their homes and go freely about their lawful business. Basically, their task is the maintenance of the Queen's Peace – that is the preservation of law and order, without these there would be anarchy. Policemen like everybody else are accountable to the law.[77]

The laws which regulate social life, then, are seen as the product of the democratic process; their interpretation is undertaken by an independent judiciary and their enforcement by an impartial police force.

Actually there is some doubt within the legal profession itself as to the precise meaning and relevance of the concept of the 'rule of law': more importantly, it does not fit the facts in Britain or America. Corruption and partiality within the police, the class bias of the judiciary, and the use of harassment, terror and violence of both a legal and illegal kind against socialists better describes the workings of the law within these societies. The 'rule of law' only has meaning when there is a period of social quiescence when democratic debate takes place within a set of assumptions that includes the sanctity of capitalistic private property. Political movements which question these views, even if not illegal, will be liable to repression. Brigadier Kitson, an important British Army theorist, in his *Low Intensity Operations* made the following comments on the way in which the law should be used during periods of social unrest:

> Broadly speaking there are two possible alternatives, the first one being that the Law should be used as just another weapon in the government's arsenal, and in this case it becomes little more than a propaganda cover for the disposal of unwanted members of the public... The other alternative is that the law should remain impartial and administer the laws of the country without any direction from the government... As a rule the second alternative is not only morally right but also expedient because it is more compatible with the government's aim of maintaining the allegiance of the population. But operating in this way can result in delays which might be impossible to accept, if, for example, it looked as if subversion was going to be used in conjunction with an orthodox invasion or the threat of one. The system might also prove unworkable if it were found to be *politically impossible to get sufficiently severe emergency regulations on to the statute book*. [emphasis added][78]

Kitson has provided a very clear statement about the provisional status of both democracy and the 'rule of law'. In this passage he does not specify who he considers to be dangerous but the nature of his own military experience and the bulk of the writings of the whole school of 'counterinsurgency' clearly make socialists the villains.

This is predictable enough; indeed, the expectation of such partiality is a lynchpin of the marxist analysis of the state, which treats the law as a class instrument used to help reproduce a social order which benefits one class over others.

To locate the role of the state within this framework requires a clarification of the concepts being used. The concept of the state itself must be in part reconsidered, and finally the relationship between crime, law and the state clarified.

9.   Marxism as a Science

In his scientific work Marx was concerned to develop concepts which would uncover the reality behind the appearance which concealed it. He did so by critically examining previous efforts to investigate economic, political and social life and demonstrating the failure of previous theorists to account for facts that they themselves would have to treat as relevant (such as what determined wages in the overall economic system) whilst at the same time demonstrating their conceptual contradictions. This can clearly be seen in his discussion of *Theories of Surplus Value* where he confronts and dialectically transcends the work of Smith and Ricardo. From his philosophical, political and economic studies, he developed the concept of the 'mode of production'. This provided the key to *reconceptualising the social world, and therefore the method by which social phenomena could be categorised according to the concepts of science rather than commonsense and pragmatic interest.* He outlined this theory in the following oft-quoted passage:

> In the social production which men carry on they enter into definite relations that are indispensable and independent of their will; these relations of production correspond to a definite stage of development of their material powers of production. The sum total of these relations of production constitutes the economic structure of society, the real foundation on which rise legal and political superstructures, and to which correspond definite forms of social consciousness . . . At a certain stage of their

development, the material productive forces of society come into conflict with the existing relations of production, or – what is but a legal expression of the same thing – with the property relations within which they had been at work before. From forms of development of the forces of production these relations turn into their fetters. Then comes the period of social revolution. With the change of the economic foundation the entire immense superstructure is more or less rapidly transformed. In considering such transformations the distinction should always be made between the material transformation of the economic conditions of production which can be determined with the precision of natural science, and the legal, political, religious, aesthetic or philosophic – in short ideological forms in which men become conscious of this conflict and fight it out.[79]

The concept of mode of production is central to any marxist analysis, including that of the state. Marx made this point when he wrote that:

The specific economic form, in which unpaid surplus-labour is pumped out of direct producers, determines the relationship of rulers and ruled …It is always the direct relationship of the owners of production to the direct producers – a relation always naturally corresponding to a definite stage in the development of the methods of labour and thereby its social productivity – which reveals the innermost secret, the hidden basis of the entire social structure, and with it the political form of the relation of sovereignty and dependence, in short, the corresponding specific form of the state.[80]

Capital was devoted to the analysis of the 'capitalist mode of production', a system in which the free labourer sells his labour-power to others, capitalists, who own the means of production from which he, the direct producer, has been separated. Having no means of subsistence he is forced to sell his labour-power on the market but receives from the employer less than the value of the commodities that he has produced: he only receives a wage sufficient to buy the commodities necessary to reproduce his labour-power, the additional value created by his labour being appropriated as surplus value – as rent, interests and profit. This is the fundamental process within capitalism but its practical realisation depends upon complex institutional arrangements and conditions which will vary depending on the development of the economy in question.

In his analysis of commodities, Marx takes these every-day objects, seemingly devoid of any mystery, and shows how complex they really are. He points out that 'a definite social relation between men…assumes, in their eyes, the fantastic form of a relation between things…'[81]

Through his consideration of the relationship between labour and the different forms of value embodied in commodities, the inaccuracy and ideological content of both everyday and economists' discussion of production and consumption stand revealed. This does not, however, deny their social significance, as Marx makes clear:

> ...the labour of the individual asserts itself as part of the labour of society, only by means of the relations which the act of exchange establishes directly between the products, and, indirectly, through them, between the producers. To the latter, therefore, the relations connecting the labour of one individual with that of the rest appears not as direct social relations between individuals at work, but as what they really are, material relations between persons and social relations between things.[82]

Norman Geras, in his article 'Essence and Appearance: Aspects of Fetishism in Marx's *Capital*' spells out the implications of this:

> Because the forms taken by capitalist social relations, their modes of appearance, are historically specific ones, they are puzzling forms, they contain a secret. The reasons why social relations should take such forms, rather than others, are not self-evident. It requires a work of analysis to discover them, to disclose the secret, and, in doing this, it reveals the content of these forms and the essence of these appearances, which cease thereafter to be puzzling. But this must not be regarded as a journey from illusion to reality. It is rather a process of elucidating one reality by disclosing its foundation and determination by another.[83]

Two interesting points emerge from these comments. Firstly, that the naive apprehension of reality cannot be simply ignored; we have to start somewhere, but we work upon our initial comprehension of some particular area and then transform it using abstract categories generated by a general consideration of our social existence. We then see the world in a different light.[84] Secondly, that while it is true that men misperceive the nature of social relationships, if they do not have some conception of the world and act in accord with it there would be nothing to analyse: it is the activity of man (informed by a view of the world) in relationship to other men and nature that determines history. That is the point that Marx was making when he criticised those who have

> only been able to see in history the political actions of princes and states, religious and all sorts of theoretical struggles, and in particular

54

in each historical epoch have had to share the illusion of that epoch. For instance, if an epoch imagines itself to be actuated by purely 'political' or 'religious' motives, although 'religion' and 'politics' are only forms of its true motives, the historian accepts this opinion. The 'idea', the 'conception' of these conditioned men about their real practice, is transformed into the sole, determining, active force which controls and determines their practice.[85]

It is not that religious and other motives are irrelevant but that they must be located within a whole way of life and be related to the limitations imposed by the general institutional structures and by the need for food, clothing and shelter.[86]

The social conditions under which men live determine the limits of their possible actions. The nature of group identifications and what are seen as the historical possibilities within these situations will affect the historical development of these societies.

Those who treat the subjective views held by people in situations as if they are irrelevant epiphenomena are distorting marxism. The construction of a scientific model that lays bare the unrecognised consequences of actions, and which specifies the limiting factors that structure these actions even when not consciously recognised, does not involve a denial that such a system is dependent on the actions of men.*

---

*This is to say that a great deal can be gained for marxism by a critical use of the subjectivist sociologists, of interactionism and ethnomethodology. These should not be dismissed in the way that Barry Hindess has treated ethnomethodology in *The Use of Official Statistics: A Critique of Positivism and Ethnomethodology*, London: Macmillan 1973. He argues that knowledge of the actor's point of view is irrelevant for scientific analysis. In order to make his point he uses an economic example – the problems associated with defining the nature of the employment of people in the census in India; this is itself dishonest since much of ethnomethodologists' work has focused on the interactions between powerful law enforcement personnel and deviants, and where they have shown quite clearly that there is very little shared understanding between the deviant and the police and/or with the researcher for that matter (see particularly Aaron Cicourel, *The Social Organisation of Juvenile Justice*, New York: Wiley 1968). More importantly he ignores the way in which the census-takers rely on their own commonsense understanding of the world to decide what people are doing and how to describe their economic activity. The degree of cross-cultural understanding of such things that does exist is due to the dependence that we share on our ability to use and combat nature. On similar points see Stephen Toulmin, *Human Understanding*, New York: Oxford University Press 1972, p.492 and Henry C.Elliott, 'Similarities and Differences between

55

10. The State within a Marxist Framework[87]

The operation of capitalism is not an expression of 'natural' laws nor is it self-evidently the best way to provide for the necessities of life. The creation of capitalism and its maintenance has required continuous effort.[88] This has involved the transformation of *all social institutions* to make them compatible with it and *the transformation of the consciousness and the conditions of existence of those who live within such societies.*

> For the conversion of his money into capital, therefore, the owner of money must meet in the market with the free labourer, free in the double sense, that as a free man he can dispose of his labour-power as his own commodity, and that on the other hand he has no other commodity for sale, is short of everything necessary for the realisation of his labour-power... One thing however is clear – Nature does not produce on the one side owners of money or commodities, and on the other men possessing nothing but their own labour-power. This relation has no natural basis neither is its social basis one that is common to all historical periods. It is clearly the result of a past historical development...[89]

Economic laws are not simply 'laws of nature' but depend on maintaining social relationships in a particular 'artificial state', itself a complex process. Marx has made clear how important is the condition both of the means of production and of those who work them for the continual reproduction of capitalism.

> Capitalist production therefore, of itself reproduces the separation between labour-power and the means of labour. It therefore reproduces and perpetuates the condition for exploiting the labourer. It incessantly forces him to sell his labour-power in order to live, and enables the capitalist to purchase labour-power in order that he may enrich himself.
> Capitalist production, therefore, under its aspect of a continuous connected process, of a process of reproduction, produces not only commodities, not only surplus-value, but also produces and reproduces the capitalist relation; on the one side the capitalist, on the other the wage-labourer.[90]

Labour-power must be 'free' to move according to the dictates of the profit imperatives of capitalism; that is to say

Science and Common Sense' in Roy Turner (ed.), *Ethnomethodology*, Harmondsworth: Penguin 1974.

that the overall forms of social organisation by which workers live their lives must not, *in aggregate*, run counter to the interests of capital. Also, what constitutes adequate reproduction of labour-power will depend upon the overall development and organisation of capitalism at any one time (laisser-faire, monopoly, national, corporate, etc.) and the specific needs of the different industries.

In nineteenth-century England, the major demand was for large numbers of unskilled workers for the labour-intensive industries. Under these conditions Marx's formula was that the minimum limit of the value of labour-power was 'determined by the value of commodities, without the daily supply of which the labourer cannot renew his vital energy, consequently by the value of those means of subsistence that are physically indispensable.'[91]

During the early twentieth-century – with the development of more capital-intensive production and the acute rivalry with Germany – the situation changed. The simple workings of the market were no longer sufficient to produce adequate labour-power. Therefore:

> Newspapers, tracts and government reports all argued that a major goal of social policy should be the production of *healthy, loyal and obedient* workers and soldiers. The moral disciplinary significance of Christianity, mainly for the working class, was already recognised, now the importance of the family for health was stressed. Social Security legislation was passed which strengthened the family, *The Old Age Pensions Act* (1903) and the *National Insurance Act* (1911).[92]

The capitalist mode of production requires an obedient work force, and the protection of the means of production under its control. How this is achieved will depend upon the stage of development of the consciousness and social organisation of the dispossessed groups within society. The state can be used to maintain discipline, but it is only one method. Both its importance and the ways it is used – repressively, organisationally or ideologically – will depend upon the specific conditions to be found within each society.

In the nineteenth-century state power was captured by the industrial bourgeoisie in order on the one hand to ensure the more efficient pacification of those inimical to the development of capitalism – achieved by using an increasingly mobile army and through the creation of the British police – and on the other to limit state interference with the economy: 'in a society with capitalist production, anarchy in the social division of labour and despotism in that of the workshop mutually condition each other'.[93]

As the century ran its course and the proletariat became better organised and potentially revolutionary the bourgeoisie sought a more general social discipline – they wanted to secure the proletariat's loyalty and obedience as total men, citizens. They attacked and destroyed Chartism because it demanded parliamentary representation on the working class's terms, and then allowed a very gradual political involvement on their own terms, through their own parties. Bagehot advised the ruling class to avoid

> ...not only every evil, but every appearance of evil; while they still have the power they must remove not only every actual grievance but, where it is possible, every seeming grievance too; they must willingly concede every claim which they can safely concede in order that they may not have to concede unwillingly some claim which would impair the safety of the country.[94]

State institutions are not separate from society, over and above it, but are an integral part of the mode of production although their role and relative importance may vary under different conditions. The state apparatuses have been developed as instruments of ruling-class interests and cannot simply be treated as tools – to be taken over by this or that group.

> Society thus far, based upon class antagonisms, had need of the state, that is, of an organisation of the particular class, which was pro tempore the exploiting class, for the maintenance of its external conditions of production, and therefore, especially for the purpose of forcibly keeping exploited the exploited classes in the condition of oppression corresponding with the given mode of production (slavery, serfdom, wage-labour). The state was the official representative of society as a whole; the gathering of it together into a visible embodiment. But it was this only insofar as it was the state of that class which itself represented, for the time being, society as a whole: in ancient times the state of slave-owning citizens; in the Middle Ages, the feudal Lords; in our time, the bourgeoisie.[95]

There is a danger, of course, of presenting an oversimplified view. Within democracies the state does not represent ruling-class interests in a simple fashion – there are opposition parties: politics is not simply a charade. Nevertheless the state cannot simply be taken over and used for socialist ends. Whilst it is true that the 'new society grows in the womb of the old' and that some state institutions can be used as a focus for revolutionary activities – overall they must be destroyed or neutralised to make possible a situation of dual power. This is the clear import of Marx's remarks about the Paris Commune:

> The working class cannot simply lay hold on to the ready-made state machinery and wield it for their own purpose. The political instrument of their enslavement cannot serve as the political instrument of their emancipation.[96]

11. The State and Substantive Analysis

Although here the focus is on state and government it is to be remembered that the ruling class does not simply work through these institutions but also has at its disposal other means, from the media to neo-fascist or gangster-based organisations.

In Western democracies the political system is the means by which 'an economically dominant class rules through democratic institutions rather than by way of dictatorship'.[97] Naked unmediated rule is usually unwelcome to the bourgeoisie. Marx, in his analysis of the Eighteenth Brumaire of Louis Bonaparte, wrote:

> The Parliamentary Republic makes their rule complete, true enough, but at the same time undermines its...foundation, since they must now confront the subjugated classes and contend against them without mediations, without the distraction of minor and subordinate struggles. It is a feeling of weakness that causes them to recoil from the *pure conditions* of their own class rule, to yearn after the less complete, more undeveloped and precisely, on that account, less *dangerous* forms of this rule.[98]

Elsewhere, Marx characterises France's Second Empire of the 1830s in a way which would fit any modern imperialist state:

> The Empire [had] the coup d'etat for its certificate of birth, universal suffrage for its sanction, and the sword for its sceptre. It professed to save the working class by breaking down Parliamentarianism [clearly limited in France to the propertied] and, with it, the undisguised subservience of government to the propertied classes. It professed to rest upon the *peasantry*, the large mass of producers not directly involved in the struggle between capital and labour. It professed to save the propertied classes

by upholding their economic supremacy over the working class. And, finally, it professed to *unite all classes* by reviving for all the chimera of national glory.[99]

Capitalist democracy is provisional, and, even when tolerated, is very limited. With the growth of working-class involvement, control of the government was moved from parliament to party, thence to the Cabinet or, as is sometimes argued, to the Prime Minister. It is less and less subject to collective control. Moreover:

> The executive authority of government itself is limited in respect of the other state institutions, whose policy and practice more often than not lie outside of direct governmental control. The government therefore does not control the state, rather the institutions making up the state – of which government is one – act together in commanding state power.[100]

These other institutions – the judiciary, the police, the army, etc. – often have quite a high degree of independence from the government. But, this does not mean that they are autonomous. The institutional and personal nexuses within which they are located guarantee that their personnel are committed to the interests of capitalism, and whatever political party is in power institutional inertia acts against social change. This is not to say that practical politics are irrelevant but reformist political programmes and even institutional changes must be related to the actual effect they have on the overall functionings of capitalism. In Britain, for example, part of the Labour Party's nationalisation programme of the 1940s was reversed by the next Tory administration. Those industries left nationalised – particularly coal mining and the railways – functioned to provide capitalism with relatively efficient and cheap fuel and transportation (private enterprise is still effectively subsidised by the coal industry) and the compensation paid to the previous owners released capital that was invested more profitably elsewhere.[101] At the same time,

> If a healthy literate working class is needed by the system then there is an objective overlap of interests between sections of the working class and the capitalist class. Furthermore, even the most reformist trade union leaders subscribe to the need for these 'improvements' for their members. In situations where there is an extension of state and municipal control over education, housing, etc., the trade union leader can play an important (although structurally marginal) role in the decisions made by these

bodies in the municipal-welfare state. They can do so without needing to change the nature of society.[102]

Social-democratic parties based on sections of the trade-union bureaucracies pose little danger to ruling-class power. Nevertheless, efforts may be made to destroy them as in Britain in 1931, and under fascism in Germany and Italy, or to pre-empt their development, which was attempted successfully in the USA.

These considerations underline the complex meaning of the statement that 'the executive of the modern state is but a committee for managing the common affairs of the whole bourgeoisie'.[103] The group actually holding the reins of government may not be ruling the country. Those ruling the country may only be holding power in the interests of some other group, the hegemonic fraction of the ruling class.

> By reigning class or fraction is meant that one from which the upper personnel of the state apparatuses is recruited, i.e. its political personnel in the broad sense. This class or fraction may be distinct from the hegemonic class or fraction. Marx gives us a prime example in the case of Britain at the end of the last century. There the hegemonic class fraction was the financial (banking) bourgeoisie, while the upper personnel in the administration, army, diplomatic corps, etc. was recruited from within the aristocracy which thus occupied the position of reigning class.[104]

The state is an essential part of the mode(s) of production found within any society. Its objective function is to help guarantee the reproduction of the economic system. It will not be the only nexus of institutions responsible for this task nor will its functionaries necessarily be the major beneficiaries of the system it protects. Similarly complex are the relationships between law making, interpretation and implementation.

12. Crime, Law and the State

Marx and Engels did not write a great deal on the subject of law and crime. In his youthful dialogue with Hegel, Marx spent some time considering the state and law and in his later works he made occasional references to both crime and the 'criminal classes'.[105] Engels made some insightful comments on the connection between criminal behaviour and the brutalising

61

effects of capitalism in *The Condition of the Working Class in England* (1845) but otherwise was not too interested in the subject. The same is true of most marxist scholars.[106] The reason for this lack of interest has been well put by Paul Hirst:

> There is no marxist theory of deviance, either in existence, or which can be developed within orthodox marxism. Crime and deviance vanish into the general theoretical concerns and the specific scientific object of marxism. Crime and deviance are no more a scientific field for marxism than education, the family or sport. The objects of marxist theory are specified by its own concepts: the mode of production, the class struggle, the state, ideology, etc.[107]

Crime and deviance are not considered by marxists to be things in themselves. It is true that in society they are generally viewed in this way but the criteria for categorising phenomena are given by the science of marxism not by everyday understandings. Marxism shows the interdependence of seemingly separate institutions such as religion, law and the economy, and questions the validity of the separate disciplines of economics, politics, sociology and criminology.

Hirst argues that crimes are activities that interfere with the effective functioning of the society as a whole. This explains the development of social control bureaucracies:

> The policeman, a state functionary, is necessary for the reproduction of capitalist social relations; he protects the property of capitalists and others, and secures certain of the conditions of labour discipline.[108]

This is unobjectionable. But elsewhere Hirst seems to accept the general social evaluation of the criminal:

> 'Crime' is defined by state law and detected and punished by the state repressive apparatus. Marx regards the state as an instrument of class oppression, an instrument which intervenes in the class struggle on behalf of the ruling class and against the proletariat and its allies. The state intervenes in the class struggle with its ideological and repressive apparatus to break the power of the political movement of the workers by means of legal and extra-legal santions. One form of such state intervention is the stigmatisation of political opponents of the bourgeoisie as 'criminals'. To stigmatise political opponents as 'common criminals' is to deny ideologically their political character and aims, to castigate them as bandits and adventurers.[109]

Elsewhere Hirst agrees with Marx and Engels' negative assessment of the lumpenproletariat and of the 'delinquent solution'. By doing so he fails to recognise the complex problems posed for monopoly capital by even a limited democracy and underestimates the important stabilising role for capitalism played by ideology and by the institutions embodying such ideology. That is, certain forms of crime and deviance are stigmatised to negate their potential for undermining social practices supportive of capitalism such as the family, the work ethic, etc.

I have already discussed the important ideological function of the concept of the 'rule of law'. To recapitulate, this claims that the legal system is an expression of the people's will; that the meaning of the law is interpreted by an independent judiciary; and that the laws are impartially enforced by an apolitical police force whose *modus operandi* is legally circumscribed. How well does this fit reality and what conclusions can be drawn from an investigation of the concrete operation of the law?[110]

This system of ideas can only have wide social currency while it seems to fit the facts. The majority of laws in Britain and America work in favour of capitalists, yet many laws do also benefit the other social classes, not only because the system needs a healthy, safe population of producers and consumers but also because it needs their loyalty. The role of the police must be understood in this context, as Mike Hayes shows:

> The British bourgeoisie [produced] a brilliantly sophisticated organisation of social control enshrouded within a masterly and deeply mystifying ideology which for so long has succeeded in masking the hidden reality of the police for *all* classes most of the time. The unarmed, friendly constable, helping the aged and the young and those in distress; the determined but scrupulous pursuer of the offender; the 'neutral' protector of life and property, using a minimum of violence and intelligent crime prevention techniques in the 'general interest'. All these and more have been and still are, dominant images of our police, *lived as real by most people most of the time*. Such images persist because they have a certain truth for all class actors in the English social formation. We cannot wish that truth away. It exists historically. But it is not the whole truth, for there is another reality and that is the structural relation of the police to our society, i.e. a Repressive State Apparatus which helps to maintain and reproduce a capitalist mode of production.[111]

In a democracy there is always the possibility that laws will be passed which are against the interests of members of the ruling class. Generally, they manage to keep their anti-social acts hidden from public scrutiny, or, failing that, have them dealt with administratively, but sometimes their acts become liable to criminal action – e.g. offences against factory safety regulations, income tax evasion or involvement with corruption. In these cases, both in Britain and America, little is done although

> The state may be pressured either nominally or effectively to prosecute the wealthy if their criminal practices become so egregiously offensive that their victims may move to overthrow the system itself.[112]*

The organisation, control and priorities established for the police, and the professional culture and affiliations of the judiciary make consistent effort in that direction very rare. This cannot be explained by reference to the lawful exercise of discretion by the police. In America illegitimate neglect of criminal activities may involve the offence of 'malfeasance' and in Britain the police have a duty to enforce the law which they can be compelled to perform.

There can be no debate about the illegality of the alliances between criminals and state bureaucracies in America and on occasion in Britain (e.g. Churchill's use of Havelock Wilson, racketeer President of the National Sailor's and Firemen's Unions). Hirst's failure to investigate concrete state practices leads him to underestimate the ideological nature and mystifying functions of bourgeois appeals to law and order.

The police tend to be either conservative or explicitly right-

---

*See essay in Part 2 on 'Corporate Crime and American Society'. Adequate research on this area is still lacking for Britain. Yet it is indicative that in 1948 the Inspectors for the Inland Revenue claimed 'that half a year's revenue [i.e. at the time £743 million] is awaiting collection if evasion could be detected and arrests vigorously pursued'. In 1966, 11,500 cases of tax evasion were completed. A further 9,300 cases were deferred due to pressure of work on the officials concerned; in 1969, 9,000 cases were completed and 3,100 deferred. Out of 115,000 known tax-evaders over the decade 1959-68, 176 were prosecuted. The Inland Revenue Staff's Federation have repeatedly asked for more manpower to tackle this problem. Instead, Sir Keith Joseph instigated the Fisher Report, and the numbers of supplementary benefits special investigators were greatly increased. In 1971 there were over 9,000 *known* cases of tax fraud which cost the Exchequer nearly £12 million. In 1971, 5,753 claimants were prosecuted for 'abusing' their benefit; the sum involved was less than £300,000. Even when prosecuted tax evaders are well treated. In one case in 1960, for example, six jewellers who in ten years defrauded the Inland Revenue of £31,000 were, on conviction, instructed to pay back the money and given the *choice* of imprisonment *or* paying fines. See Frank Pearce, 'The Rule of Law: A Bourgeois Myth', *Writing on the Wall*, no. 1.

wing, affiliations that are usually ignored whereas left-wing tendencies – rare as they are – will soon be suppressed.[113] This has been particularly true during periods of class and racial conflict. The judiciary has shown similar partiality in its interpretation of the law in anti-socialist directions.

I have already mentioned Kitson's comments on the 'rule of law'. His work is now reasonably well known. What is not so well known is the complex legal position of the army. The frequent celebration of Britain's lack of a written constitution ignores the extent to which this allows hundreds of years of pre-democratic political and legal practice to determine much of British law. There has never been any doubt about the political affiliations of the officers in the British army – they are and always have been profoundly conservative. Their loyalty, it is argued by military law, is not to the government but to the Crown. The implications are profound. Soldiers, as the *Manual of Military Law* makes clear, are in a special position during disturbances:

> Though there is no legal difference between soldiers and other citizens in respect of the duty to respond to the call of the civil authority, there is, in the cases of disturbance where the civil authority has not asked for help, a duty to take action laid upon the military commanders by the Queen's Regulations which is not laid upon other citizens, except magistrates and peace officers and *even though the civil authority should give directions to the contrary* the commander of the troops, if it is really necessary, is *bound* to take such action as the circumstances demand.[114]

Socialism is seen as the major danger. Obviously, if there were disturbances because of right-wing opposition to left-wing legislative proposals or legislation any 'civil order' established would be repressive and reactionary. The Labour Party recognised this danger in the thirties and discussed bringing in special legislation if they were to come to office.[115]

A consideration of legal practice and social conflict makes clear the precise meaning of the 'rule of law'. It also suggests that an adequate understanding of the operation of the law requires some acquaintance with concrete historical situations and not simply a reliance on somewhat abstract formulations derived from marxist theory.

The operation of the state's repressive apparatus is not

simply determined by considerations of legality or illegality. Not all criminals need concern themselves overmuch with the law (e.g. some white-collar criminals); at the same time certain law-abiding citizens are subject to the attentions of this repressive apparatus. The criterion for state intervention is the extent to which activities undermine the social order. The conventional presentation of this social order is ideological – in the sense that it describes, in a partial manner, the workings of the society whilst at the same time masking the 'real' nature of the social order. A recognition of the distinction between the imaginary and real social orders is fundamental to understanding the actual *modus operandi* of the repressive apparatus. According to the 'imaginary social order' Britain and America are societies where the people have freely chosen via the democratic processes to have a free enterprise system humanised by elements of a mixed economy. The 'real social order' is a monopoly capitalist system, with a certain degree of state control of the industrial infrastructure, but where the state itself is ultimately dominated by the ruling class.

The system is not maintained by force alone. The important legitimating functions of the 'imaginary social order' have already been commented on. Moreover laws are but one and a very formalised expression of the 'rules' regulating the way of life that the ruling class considers appropriate for members of society. Such rules are communicated and institutionalised in the everyday practices of ordinary people through the 'ideological apparatus' – the family, the educational system, the media, etc. They are important for the maintenance of the attitudes and forms of life compatible with capitalism and require the control, and if possible the elimination, of rival 'life styles'. The suggestion that the life of the 'average' Briton or American is normal and natural and the depiction of other possibilities as animalistic, immature, corrupt or foreign provides one mechanism of control. The strategy of stressing the normality of certain ways of life and the abnormality of others is an important function of the ideological apparatus. In practice, misrepresentation, invective, harassment and repression are usually found together. There may be a variety of justifications for such activities. In 1954 Richard Nixon for example, speaking in Denver Colorado, claimed that:

Ninety-six per cent of the 6,926 Communists, fellow travellers, sex perverts, people with criminal records, dope addicts, drunks and other security risks removed under the Eisenhower security program were hired by the Truman administration.[116]

Homosexuality calls into question the naturalness of family institutions; drug usage and its attendant 'expressive' culture can undermine the division of social time into work and earned leisure. Deviance can help fracture the massiveness of hegemonic domination over all aspects of life,[117] thus revealing the inhumanity of capitalism which can only survive by truncating the potential of those under its sway. As opposed to this, socialism promises a truly free existence: it would involve

the abolition of these inequitable property relationships revealed in the state and would deny the authority of any narrow interest to enforce its claims over any one form of divergent behaviour. In that sense, diversity would be institutionalised in a community rather than being defined as crime, and segregated off, by a power-invested state. Under real Socialism diversity would be freed from the forces of all but communal restraint.[118]

An economically, socially, sexually and racially liberated socialist society would have practical democracy operating within work, education and all other institutions. But this is no more inevitable than is revolution itself. It can only come about if a commitment to liberation in all these ways is part of the programme and practice of those committed to revolutionary change. Thus certain kinds of deviant activity[119] have within themselves a positive potential for social change and for that reason are viewed so negatively by the agents of social control. The traditional marxist attitude towards the lumpenproletariat can be seen as reflecting at best a situational wisdom derived from an analysis of a specific society, and, at worst, a narrow and crippled vision of socialism. (The lumpenproletariat may not be very trustworthy allies but how reliable are middle class converts to socialism?)

This discussion of bourgeois and marxist ways of approaching crime and deviance has shown that the only way to understand the actual workings of social control mechanisms within capitalism is to recognise that they are directed against those activities which threaten its effective reproduction, as it really is, in all

67

its naked barbarity. The indifference shown to the sufferings of the 'lumpenproletariat' and the limited attention paid to the health and welfare of the productive working class, while mystifying and oppressing them both, stands in stark contrast to the protection afforded the ruling class and its possessions. Marxism in no way precludes the use of insights gained from some perceptive interactionists, yet the meaning of their ideas is thereby changed, because they have been incorporated into a system of thought capable of analysing the totality of the social world and dedicated to its transformation.

Notes

1. See particularly F. Ivan Nye and James F. Short, 'Reported Behavior as a Criterion of Deviant Behavior', *Social Problems*, 5, pp.207-13, 1957, and the references and discussion in Steven Box, *Deviance, Reality and Society*, London: Holt Rinehart & Winston 1971, ch.3. See also A. Cicourel and John Kitsuse, *The Educational Decision Makers*, Indianapolis: Bobbs-Merrill 1963; Nathan Goldmann, *The Differential Selection of Juvenile Offenders for Court Appearance*, National Research and Information Center, National Council on Crime and Delinquency, 1963; and Michael Phillipson, *Sociological Aspects of Crime and Delinquency*, London: Routledge & Kegan Paul 1971. On the processes within the court system see William Chambliss, *Crime and the Legal Process*, New York: McGraw-Hill 1969, part II.

2. See Courtland C. Van Vechten, 'Differential Criminal Case Mortality in Selected Jurisdictions', *American Sociological Review*, December 1942, 7, pp.833-9 and Paul Wiles, 'Criminal Statistics and Sociological Explanations of Crime', in W.G. Carson and Paul Wiles, *Crime and Delinquency in Britain*, London: Martin Robertson 1971.

3. Howard S. Becker, 'Labelling Theory Reconsidered', in Paul Rock and Mary McIntosh (eds.), *Deviance and Social Control*, London: Tavistock 1974, p.45.

4. Edwin Lemert, *Human Deviance, Social Problems and Social Control*, New York: Prentice-Hall 1967, p.5.

5. George Herbert Mead, *Mind, Self and Society*, London: University of Chicago Press 1962 (first published 1934) p.301.

6. See particularly George Herbert Mead, *op.cit.*; Anselm Strauss (ed.), *George Herbert Mead on Social Psychology*, Chicago: University of Chicago Press; C.W. Morris (ed.), *The Philosophy of the Act by George Herbert Mead*, Chicago: University of Chicago Press 1938; John W. Petras (ed.), *George Herbert Mead: Essays on His Social Philosophy*, New York: Teachers College Press 1968; George Herbert Mead, *Selected Writings*, Indianapolis: Bobbs-Merrill 1964. Assessments can be found in Maurice Natanson, *The Social Dynamics of George Herbert Mead*, Washington DC: Public Affairs Press 1956, and Richard Lichtman, 'Symbolic Interactionism and Social Reality: Some Marxist Queries', *Berkeley Journal of Sociology*, 15. Some of his other work was very different from that primarily relied upon by the authors examined here: e.g. Merritt H. Moore (ed.), George Herbert Mead *The Philosophy of the Present*, Chicago: Open

Court Publishing 1932. See the comments made by Peter McHugh in his *Defining the Situation*, Indianapolis: Bobbs-Merrill 1968, ch.3.

7. Herbert Blumer, *Symbolic Interactionism*, Boston: Allyn & Bacon 1967; Everett Hughes, *Men and Their Work*, Glencoe: Free Press 1958; Arnold Rose, *Human Behavior and Social Processes*, Boston: Houghton Mifflin 1962, a book of readings; other such readers include Jerome G. Manis and Bernard N. Meltzer, *Symbolic Interaction: A Reader in Social Psychology*, Boston: Allyn & Bacon 1967; Chad Gordon and Kenneth J. Gergen, *The Self in Social Interaction*, New York: John Wiley 1968.

8. Good selections of such writings can be found in Earl Rubington and Kirson S. Weinberg, *Deviance: The Interactionist Perspective*, New York: MacMillan 1968, and Howard Becker (ed.), *The Other Side: Perspectives on Deviance*, New York: Free Press 1964; see also, S. Cohen (ed.), *Images of Deviance*, Harmondsworth: Penguin 1971; Ian Taylor and Laurie Taylor (eds.), *Politics and Deviance*, Harmondsworth: Penguin 1973.

9. Of special note are Ian Taylor, Paul Walton and Jock Young, *The New Criminology*, London: Routledge & Kegan Paul 1973, ch.5; Milton Mankoff, 'Societal Reaction and Career Deviance: A Critical Analysis', *Sociological Quarterly*, 12, Spring; Alexander Liazos, 'The Poverty of the Sociology of Deviance: Nuts, Sluts and Perverts', *Social Problems* 20, (1972). Additional critical comments are to be found in Carol B. Warren and John N. Johnson, 'A Critique of Labelling Theory from the Phenomenological Perspective', in Robert A. Scott and Jack D. Douglas (eds.), *Theoretical Perspectives on Deviance*, New York: Basic Books 1972; Don H. Zimmerman and D. Lawrence Wieder, 'Ethnomethodology and the Problems of Order: Comment on Denzin', in Jack Douglas (ed.), *Understanding Everyday Life*, London: Routledge & Kegan Paul 1971; Jeff Coulter, *Approaches to Insanity: A Philosophical and Sociological Study*, London: Martin Robertson 1972; Mike Phillipson and Maurice Roche, 'Phenomenology, Sociology and the Study of Deviance', in Paul Rock and Mary McIntosh (eds.), *Deviance and Social Control*, London: Tavistock 1974.

10. Edwin Lemert, *Social Pathology*, New York: McGraw-Hill 1951, p.23.

11. Edwin Lemert, *op.cit.*, 1967, p.25.

12. On 'middle range theory' see Robert K. Merton, *Social Theory and Social Structure*, New York: Free Press 1957, chs.2 and 3.

13. Edwin Lemert, *op.cit.*, 1951, p.23.

14. *ibid.*, pp.33, 207, 211, 280.

15. *ibid.*, p.175.

16. *ibid.*, p.188.

17. *ibid.*, p.190.

18. *ibid.*, p.225, see also p.176.

19. *ibid.*, p.208.

20. *ibid.*, p.182.

21. *ibid.*, p.210.

22. *ibid.*, p.197.

23. *ibid.*, pp.213-21.

24. *ibid.*, p.207.

25. *ibid.*, pp.204-5.

26. *ibid.*, p.202.

27. *ibid.*, p.202.

28. *ibid.*, p.211. See also 'Beyond Mead: The Societal Reaction to Deviance', *Social Problems*, Vol.12, no.4, April 1974, p.458, where he uses similar ideas.

29. Paul Walton, 'The Case of the Weathermen: Societal Reaction and Radical

Commitment', in Ian Taylor and Laurie Taylor (eds.), *Politics and Deviance*, Harmondsworth: Penguin 1973, p.158.

30. Edwin Lemert, *op.cit.*, 1951, p.106. See the discussion in Tony Woodiwiss, 'Law, labour and the State in the United States', in Mike Hayes and Frank Pearce (eds.), *Crime, Law and the State*, London: Routledge & Kegan Paul 1976.

31. Edwin Lemert, *op.cit.*, 1951, p.106.

32. *ibid.*, p.189.

33. *ibid.*, p.181.

34. James Weinstein, *The Decline of American Socialism 1912-25*, New York: Monthly Review Press 1967, pp.53-63.

35. See in particular James Weinstein, 1967, Weinstein's discussion of the literature on socialism, 'Socialism's Hidden Heritage', and other essays in James Weinstein and David W. Eakins (eds.), *For a New America*, New York: Random House 1970. See also Melvin Dubofsky, *We Shall be All*, Chicago: Quadrangle Books 1969; Jeremy Brecher, *Strike*, San Francisco: Straight Arrow Books 1972; Art Preis, *Labor's Giant Step*, New York: Pathfinder Press 1972; see also material published in *Socialist Revolution* and *Radical America*, and references in the essay on organised crime, Staughton Lynd, *The Intellectual Origins of American Radicalism*, New York: Vintage 1969; David Harris, *Socialist Origins in the United States*, Amsterdam: International Institute for Study of Social History by Van Gorcum & Co., Netherlands 1966; Charles Nordhoff, *The Communistic Societies of the United States*, Toronto: Dover 1966 (first edition 1875).

36. Edwin Lemert, *op.cit.*, 1951, pp.202-3.

37. *ibid.*, p.201.

38. Gabriel Kolko, *Railroads and regulation 1877-1916*, Princeton: Princeton University Press 1963 and Gabriel Kolko, *The Triumph of Conservatism*, Chicago: Quadrangle books 1965; James Weinstein, *The Corporate Ideal in the Liberal State;* Robert H. Wiebe, *The Search for Order: 1877-1920*, London: Macmillan 1967; and the essays in James Weinstein and David W. Eakins, *For a New America*, New York: Random House 1970; Tony Woodiwiss, *op.cit.*

39. David Horowitz, *Empire and Revolution*, New York: Vintage Books 1969.

40. G. William Domhoff, *Who Rules America?* Englewood Cliffs: Prentice-Hall 1967, pp.75-6.

41. J. Edgar Hoover, 'The Faith of Free Men', in Richard Knudten (ed.), *Criminological Controversies*, New York: Appleton-Century-Crofts 1968, pp.6-7.

42. Edwin Lemert, *op.cit.*, 1967, p.21.

43. *ibid.*, p.10.

44. *ibid.*, p.15.

45. See his comments in *op.cit.*, 1967, p. v., and in the 1972 edition of the same book, the new article, 'Social Problems and the Sociology of Deviance', p.22.

46. Edwin Lemert, *op.cit.*, 1967, p.15.

47. *ibid.*, p.11.

48. *ibid.*, p.11.

49. Karsten Struhl, 'From Civil Disobedience to Revolution', unpublished paper, Department of Philosophy, Long Island University, New York, USA.

50. Stuart L. Hills, *Crime, Power and Morality*, Scranton: Chandler 1971, p.6.

51. Nelson Polsby, *Community Power and Political Theory*, New Haven: Yale University Press 1963, p.118.

52. Todd Gittlin, 'Local Pluralism as Theory and Ideology', *Studies on the Left* 1965, reprinted in Hans P. Dreitzel (ed.), *Recent Sociology*, no.1, London:

Macmillan 1969, p.64.

53. Edwin Lemert, *op.cit.*, 1974, p.465.

54. Peter Bachrach and Morton S. Baratz, 'Two Faces of Power', *The American Political Science Review*, Vol. 56, no.4, December 1962.

55. Edward Banfield, *Political Influence*, New York: Free Press 1961; Robert Dahl, *Who Governs?* New Haven: Yale University Press 1961.

56. Todd Gittlin, *op.cit.*, pp.70-7.

57. Tony Woodiwiss, 'Post-Behaviouralism: A Marxist View of a Revolution in Political Science', unpublished paper.

58. Howard S. Becker, *op.cit.*, 1963, pp.17-18; see also Richard Quinney, 'Crime in Political Perspective', *American Behavioral Scientist*, 8 December 1964, pp.19-22.

59. Howard S. Becker, 'Whose Side are we On?', *Social Problems*, 14, Winter 1967, pp.239-47. Reprinted in Larry T. Reynolds and Janice M. Reynolds, *The Sociology of Sociology*, New York: David McKay 1970, pp.207-11.

60. Howard S. Becker and Irving Louis Horowitz, introduction to *Campus Power Struggles*, New York: Transaction Books 1970.

61. Peter Bachrach and Morton S. Baratz, *Power and Poverty: Theory and Practice*, New York: Oxford University Press 1970, pp.201-13.

62. *ibid.*, p.205.

63. Tony Woodiwiss, *op.cit.*, p.27.

64. Edward Hayes, *Power Structure and Urban Policy: Who Rules in Oakland?*, New York: McGraw-Hill 1972, p.194.

65. *ibid.*, p.199.

66. Howard S. Becker, 'Labelling Theory Reconsidered', in Paul Rock and Mary McIntosh (eds.), *Deviance and Social Control*, London: Tavistock 1974.

67. Robert H. Wiebe, *The Search for Order: 1877-1920*, London: Macmillan 1967, pp.146-7.

68. George Herbert Mead, 'The Working Hypothesis in Social Reform', in John W. Petras (ed.), *George Herbert Mead: Essays on his Social Philosophy*, New York: Teachers College Press 1968, p.127.

69. Tony Platt, 'The Triumph of Benevolence: The Origins of Juvenile Justice System in America', mimeographed, 1972.

70. Britain, immediately prior to 1914, was riven by conflict – class, religious and the women's movement. The outbreak of the First World War swamped the realities of the societal contradictions under a stultifying blanket of jingoism; See George Dangerfield, *The Strange Death of Liberal England*, New York: Capricorn Books 1961. However the contradictions did not disappear, as was clear from the tremendous ongoing class conflict expressed, for example, in the shop stewards movement and the triple alliance; see Allen Hutt, *The Post-War History of the British Working Class*, London: Gollancz 1937, and J.T. Murphy, *Preparing for Power*, London: Pluto Press 1973. For this reason I think that Szasz's concept of 'scapegoating' with its stress on displacement, is far more accurate than those of Mead, Durkheim and Erikson. (Thomas Szasz, *The Manufacture of Madness*, New York: Delia Books 1970.)

71. George Herbert Mead, in John W. Petras, *op.cit.*, p.141.

72. Alexander Liazos, 'The Poverty of the Sociology of Deviance: Nuts, Sluts and Perverts,' *Social Problems*, 20 (1972).

73. Alvin Gouldner, 'Sociologist as Partisan: Sociology and the Welfare State', *The American Sociologist*, 3, May 1968, pp.103-6, reprinted in Larry T. Reynolds and Janice M. Reynolds, *op.cit.*, p.228.

74. The phrase was coined by Edwin Schur – see his *Crimes Without Victims*, Englewood-Cliffs: Prentice-Hall 1965. Compare such views and policy proposals with those in Jerome Tuccille, *Radical Libertarianism: A Right Wing Alternative*, Indianapolis: Bobbs-Merrill 1970.

75. Karl Marx and Friedrich Engels, *The German Ideology*, New York: International Publishers 1963, p.16.

76. The Departmental Committee on Section (2) of The Official Secrets Act, 1911, *Report*, Vol.1, Cmnd.5104, London: HMSO 1972, p.46.

77. Royal Commission on the Police, *Report*, Cmnd.1728, London: HMSO 1962, p.45. For discussions of it in the American context see Sandford H. Kadish, 'Legal Norm and Discretion in Police and Sentencing Processes', *Harvard Law Review*, 75, 1962, and Jerome H. Skolnick, *Justice Without Trial*, New York: Wiley 1966, ch.1.

78. Frank Kitson, *Low Intensity Operation: Subversion Insurgency and Peacekeeping*, London: Faber & Faber 1971, pp.69-70. Kitson is no 'maverick'. Arguments presented by him and his co-ideologues had particularly strong support within the Heath government; see *In Defence of Peace*, London: Conservative Political Centre 1973. I have focused on Britain since the partiality of the law in America is so much more evident.

79. Karl Marx, *Critique of Political Economy* (1859) Calcutta: International Library 1904, pp.11-12. For discussion of scientificity see particularly Stephen Toulmin, *Human Understanding*, New York: Oxford University Press 1972; Stephen Toulmin, *The Philosophy of Science*, London: Grey Arrow 1962; Imre Lakatos and Alan Musgrave (eds.), *Criticism and the Growth of Knowledge*, London: Cambridge University Press 1970, and also Karl Marx, 1859, *op.cit.*

80. Karl Marx, *Capital*, Vol.3, London: Lawrence & Wishart 1971, p.791.

81. Karl Marx, *Capital*, Vol.1 (1867), London: Lawrence & Wishart 1971, p.72.

82. *ibid.*, p.73.

83. Norman Geras, 'Essence and Appearance; Aspects of Fetishism in Marx's *Capital*', *New Left Review*, 65, p.77.

84. See Karl Marx, *op.cit.*, 1859 and 1904 pp.292-305, 'The Method of Political Economy'.

85. Karl Marx and Friedrich Engels, *The German Ideology* (1846), New York: International Publishers 1947, p.30.

86. Karl Marx, *The Eighteenth Brumaire of Louis Bonaparte* (1852), Moscow: Progress Publishers 1957, p.10.

87. This discussion owes a great deal to Tom Wengraf's unpublished paper, 'Notes on Marx and Engels' Theories of the Development of the Capitalist State'.

88. See for example the discussions of the development of capitalism in Ernesto Laclau, 'Feudalism and Capitalism in Latin America', *New Left Review*, 67; Maurice Dobb, *et.al.*, 'Feudalism to Capitalism – a symposium', *Science and Society*, 1963.

89. Karl Marx, *Capital*, Vol.1, p.169. See also part 7 on 'The So-called Primitive Accumulation'.

90. *ibid.*, pp.577-8.

91. *ibid.*, p.173.

92. Frank Pearce and Andrew Roberts, 'The Social Regulation of Sexual Behaviour and the Development of Industrial Capitalism in Britain', in Roy Bailey and Jock Young (eds.), *Contemporary Social Problems in Britain*, Farnborough: D.C. Heath 1973, pp.51-72.

93. Karl Marx, *Capital*, Vol.1, p.386.

94. Walter Bagehot, *The English Constitution* (introduction to second edition)

1872.

95. Friedrich Engels, *Anti-Dühring*, Moscow: Foreign Languages Publishing House 1969, p.393.

96. Karl Marx, *The Civil War in France* (1871), Peking Foreign Languages Press 1966, pp.227-8.

97. Ralph Miliband, *The State in Capitalist Society*, London: Weidenfeld & Nicolson 1969, p.22.

98. Karl Marx, *The Eighteenth Brumaire of Louis Bonaparte*, *op.cit.*

99. Karl Marx, *The Civil War in France*, p.66. Roosevelt might also fit such a model in the American situation.

100. Tony Bunyan, *The Political Police in Britain*, London: Julian Friedmann, forthcoming.

101. Clive Jenkins, *Power at the Top*, London: MacGibbon & Kee 1959.

102. Frank Pearce, 'The British Road to Incorporation', *Writing on the Wall*, no.2, p.3.

103. Karl Marx and Friedrich Engels, *Manifesto of the Communist Party* (1848), Moscow: Foreign Languages Publishing House (n.d.), p.52.

104. Nicos Poulantzas, 'On Social Classes', *New Left Review*, 78, p.45.

105. See particularly John O'Malley (ed.), Karl Marx: *Critique of Hegel's Philosophy of Right* (1843), London: Cambridge University Press 1970. Karl Marx and Friedrich Engels, *Manifesto of the Communist Pary* (1848); Karl Marx, *Theories of Surplus Value*, Vo.1.

106. Exceptions are Willem Bonger, *Criminality and Economic Condition* (1916), Bloomington: Indiana University Press 1969; Karl Renner, *The Institutions of Private Law and their Social Functions*, London: Routledge & Kegan Paul 1949; Eric J. Hobsbawm, *Bandits*, Harmondsworth: Penguin 1972.

107. Paul Q. Hirst, 'Marx and Engels on Law, Crime and Morality', *Economy and Society*, Vol.1, no.1, February 1972, p.29.

108. *ibid.*, p.50.

109. *ibid.*, p.44.

110. The complex nature of this question was indicated by Engels: 'In a modern state, law, must not only correspond to the general economic conditions and be its expression, but it must also be an *internally coherent* expression which does not, owing to inner contradictions, reduce itself to nought. And in order to achieve this, the faithful reflection of economic conditions suffers increasingly. All the more so the more rarely it happens that a code of law is the blunt, unmitigated, unadulterated expression of the domination of a class – this in itself would offend the 'conception of right'.' Marx and Engels, *Selected Works*, London: Lawrence & Wishart 1968, p.697.

111. Mike Hayes, 'The Police and Industrial Capital', in Mike Hayes and Frank Pearce (eds.), *Crime, Law and the State*, London: Routledge & Kegan Paul 1976, p.63. While the same effort has not been made in the USA to project the police as 'friendly' their violence tends to be viewed as generalised – albeit somewhat racist – but its class connotations are almost ignored. See my comments on Lemert above and William Cook, 'Policemen in Society: Which Side are They on?', *Berkeley Journal of Sociology*.

112. David M. Gordon, 'Class and the Economics of Crime', *Review of Radical Political Economics*, Vol.3, no.5, Summer 1971, p.62.

113. See the discussion of the British police's attempts to unionise, during the immediate postwar years of 1918 and 1919 when class conflict was intense, in Vic L. Allen, 'The National Union of Police and Prison Officers', *Economic History Review*, Vol.II, no.1, 1958. For the French experience, when communists were eliminated from the CRS, see Alfred W. McCoy, *The Politics of Heroin in South East Asia*, New York: Harper & Row 1972, p.44. For Britain see Stuart Bowes, *The Police and Civil Liberties*, London: Lawrence & Wishart 1968. For America see below, 'Organised Crime in Its Historical Context'; for accounts of right-wing political organisations within the police see Jerome Skolnick, *The Politics of Protest*, New York: Simon & Schuster 1970, pp.268-92; Frank Donner, 'Political Informers' in Pat Watters and Stephen Gillers (eds.), *Investigating the FBI*, New York: Doubleday 1973, pp.350-51.

114. *Manual of Military Law*, Part I (9th edn.), London: HMSO 1964, section 5.

115. Ralph Miliband, *Parliamentary Socialism*, London: Merlin 1961, pp.193-201.

116. Quoted in Les Evans and Allen Myers, *Watergate and the Myth of American Democracy*, New York: Pathfinder 1974, p.11.

117. See Jock Young, *The Drugtakers*, London: MacGibbon & Kee 1971; Frank Pearce, 'How to be Immoral and Ill, Pathetic and Dangerous all At the Same Time! The Mass Media Treatment of Homosexuality', in Stan Cohen and Jock Young (eds.), *The Manufacture of News*, London: Constable 1973; and Dennis Altman, *Homosexuality: Oppressions and Liberation*, New York: Avon 1971.

118. Ian Taylor, Paul Walton and Jock Young, 'Rejoinder to Reviewers', in review symposium on *The New Criminology*, *British Journal of Criminology*, Vol.3, no.4, p.401.

119. Not all; some like rape must be condemned and linked with the overall structure of social relationships. Susan Griffin, 'Rape The All American Crime', *Ramparts*, reprinted in Mike Brake and Frank Pearce, *Circles and Arrows: Critical Perspectives on Human Sexuality*, forthcoming.

2.

Corporate Crime
and American Society

1. Introduction

The general public in most western countries has been made very conscious of the 'crime problem', of the need for 'law and order'. There is little doubt that the 1968 Republican campaign in America centred on this issue: in September of that year Vice-President Spiro T.Agnew said:

> When I talk about troublemakers, I'm talking about muggers and criminals in the streets, assassins of political leaders, draft evaders and flag burners, campus militants, hecklers and demonstrators against candidates for public office and looters and burners of cities.[1]

In 1965 J. Edgar Hoover, then head of the Federal Bureau of Investigation, after abusing communists turned to the crime problem which he defined in terms of the citizen's exposure to violence and theft.

> Today the onslaught continues – with five offences being recorded every minute. There is a vicious crime of violence – a murder, forcible rape or assault to kill – every two and a half minutes; a robbery each five minutes; a burglary every twenty-eight seconds; and fifty-two automobiles are stolen every hour.[2]

Crime is seen as the province of young lower-class males, particularly blacks. That this view is misleading soon becomes clear when facts bypassed or played down by opinion-formers are taken into account.

Although there is a strong emphasis placed on crimes of violence, they constituted only 13 per cent of the FBI's 'index crimes' in the Uniform Crime Report of 1965. The other 'index crimes' were thefts of various kinds – car thefts, burglaries and general larcenies; of these burglary was the most lucrative, in 1965 involving sums of $284 million, according to the FBI.[3] As against this, the President's Commission on Law Enforcement in 1967 estimated that organised crime made *a profit of $7 billion from gambling*:[4] yet the fight against organised crime has attracted little of the FBI's resources and even recent legislation purportedly aimed at it has had as the major target political radicals.

Of more immediate interest in this discussion, crimes by 'white-collar' groups are ignored by the FBI, despite the fact that the President's Commission itself said:

> There is no knowing how much embezzlement, fraud, loan sharking, and other forms of thievery from individuals or commercial institutes there is, or how much price-rigging, tax evasion, bribery graft, and other forms of thievery from the public at large there is. The Commission's studies indicate that the economic losses those crimes cause are far greater than those caused by the three Index Crimes against property.[5]

And Senator Warren Magnuson named deceptive selling as today's 'most serious form of theft, accounting for more dollars lost each year than robbery, larceny, auto thefts, embezzlement, and forgery combined'. Kolko, in his scholarly study of the distribution of wealth in American society, has shown that in 1957 at least $27·7 billion were under-reported on tax returns; most of this illegal saving was kept by the richest 10 per cent of the population.[6] Moreover, at least $11 billion of this were retained by the wealthiest 1 per cent of the American population, which owns 80 per cent of the corporate wealth. This unreported income would have been taxed at a rate of 90 cents to every dollar – which would mean that on an income of $11 billion, well over $9 billion would be owed the taxation department. The richest 1 per cent of the American people defrauded the majority of *more than $9 billion* in one year alone.

Violations of the anti-trust laws are even more important. These laws are supposed to ensure that competition keeps prices at the lowest possible level, by outlawing monopolies and by stopping firms colluding to fix prices: profits over and above those that should be made with an efficient competitive industry are illegal. The occasional prosecution under these Acts lays bare a volume of *illegal* excess profits that is staggering. In one famous case in 1961, 'The Heavy Electrical Equipment Cases', General Electric alone made at least $50 million excess profits, in this one market. Such 'business activity' is typical not only of General Electric but of large corporations in America generally.* The corporations provide the most efficient and largest examples of organised crime in America.

---

*Actionable practices by corporations are not restricted to America. In Britain, it is arguable that a *prima facie* case existed for prosecution of the Ferranti Corporation for fraud, under the precedent of ICR Haulage vs. Rex, 1943. The facts of the case are briefly as follows. In 1963 Ferranti and the Ministry of Aviation engaged in a fixed price contract

The evidence shows how inaccurate are Hoover's and Agnew's accounts of America's 'crime problem'. Using the government's own criteria of the cost of crime to the community, burglary, an 'index crime' for the FBI, is surprisingly insignificant. The $284 million worth of goods stolen in 1965 represents *only 3 per cent* of the estimated annual profits of 'organised crime' (conventionally defined), and only 3 per cent of the money gained by the tax frauds of the wealthiest 1 per cent in 1957.

This alone calls into question the justifications given for the mode and distribution of police enforcement activity and for the severity of sanctions imposed by the court. Bourgeois ideologues would answer this by talking of the 'common' good, yet the most economically significant crimes, those of the wealthy, are the least publicised, investigated and, if punished, there is little stigma attached to the known offenders. This discrepancy between theory and practice cannot be explained in terms of the unavoidable ignorance of those responsible for dealing with crime, since the figures quoted above are derived in large part from government publications. Such sources of information have been deliberately chosen and the argument has focused initially on a very legalistically defined subject-matter in order to demonstrate that the USA (and capitalist societies generally) *do not even abide by their own criteria of reasonableness*. There is a contradiction between the way things are supposed to happen

---

for the construction of missiles. The contract specified a 'fair and reasonable profit', and in fact the price and profit were only agreed upon when four-fifths of the missiles had been delivered. It was estimated that the missiles would cost £12,013,720 with a profit of £810,353, a rate of profit of 6¾ per cent on cost. A subsequent enquiry revealed that the costs had been £7,051,109 and profits £5,772,964, a rate of 82 per cent on cost. The company agreed to pay back £4,250,000, retaining an extra £650,000, giving them an actual profit rate of 21 per cent. Corporations can be prosecuted for fraud, and Ferranti and the government made these estimates at a late stage in the negotiations when Ferranti knew the wage bills were lower than estimated. Moreover as a 'fair and reasonable profit' was specified prosecution would seem to have been logical. In its absence one can only conclude that Ferranti received a £650,000 bonus for their cleverness. See Dennis Chapman, *Sociology and the Stereotype of the Criminal*, London: Tavistock 1968, p. 179; Alan Rooney, 'Aircraft and Workers Control', London, *International Socialism*, 33; L.H. Leigh, *The Criminal Liability of Corporation in English Law*, London: Weidenfeld & Nicolson 1969, p. 51.

and what actually occurs. My major aim is to explain *why* there is a discrepancy between the world (legitimate as well as criminal) portrayed by official agencies and the mass media, and that revealed by a more sophisticated socialist analysis of capitalist societies. I have restricted the analysis to America although similar points can be made about other capitalist societies.

The method that I have adopted for Part 2 of the book is first to articulate bourgeois accounts of these phenomena and then demonstrate through detailed criticism the superiority of a marxist analysis. I first examine the conventional account of the development of the major 'anti-business' legislation – the anti-trust laws – which proves incapable of explaining big business's support for and involvement in the formulation and implementation of these laws. This can only be understood by relating the goals of corporate capitalists to the changing social, political and economic environment from the latter half of the nineteenth-century to date. I then focus on a famous anti-trust prosecution in 1961 in order to try to determine how typical of businessmen were those involved. This once again raises the question of the relationship between official portrayals of reality, in this case the economic system, and what is actually taking place. In doing so, this essay will have already posed questions which are not raised by positivist criminology,[7] and will continue to do so when examining criminal activities in labour relations. It is in the discussion of the international activities of corporations that the most radical break is made with traditional criminology, for it is only by understanding why certain actions are *not* prohibited by law, either international law or by those of certain 'underdeveloped' countries, that we can make sense of the social relationships inside the capitalist world system.

Thus the ultimate implication of this mode of analysis is the dissolution of criminology as a separate discipline. In order to explain the distribution of criminal activity, and the nature of the social response to this, it proves necessary to contrast the 'imaginary' social order in America – portrayed as a pluralist, democratic, free-enterprise society, – with a more adequate (i.e. better theorised) description of its nature. This will explain certain hidden but significant social processes in capitalist societies. Furthermore, the justification for retaining capitalism in terms of its 'freedoms' will be seen as null and void, particularly when these are compared to the freedom to be found under a collective, democratic socialism.

Such an understanding allows us to see the rationality, from a bourgeois point of view, of concentrating on lower-class criminals: it is functional in maintaining the American class system. Firstly, it strengthens the dominant individualistic ideology. If the criminals are also the social failures (those at the bottom of an open, competitive, hierarchical class system, where any man can succeed), then their criminality is caused by their *inadequacies* (lack of determination, moral weakness, etc.) and the major social institutions are not exposed to critical assessment. Secondly, by defining such individuals as non-citizens with no rights to employment, education, etc. the system's failure to provide these for them (independently of their criminality) is obscured. Finally, by criminalising them and treating them as social and amoral, their potential for developing an ideologically sophisticated understanding of their situation is neutralised, and by incarcerating them it is made difficult for them to organise to realise their ideas.[8] American class society would be threatened by the development of an ideologically sophisticated 'lower-class' political movement.

Furthermore not all white-collar crimes are equally immune to prosecution. If, for example, embezzlement was left unprosecuted and there was a large increase in such activity, capitalism might well collapse; for the financial transactions essential to this kind of economy inevitably involve trust but cannot take place in a manner which gives fool-proof protection from violations of it. It is necessary to investigate the social effects of these crimes. Thus, in the Second World War it was imperative that the state should succeed in stopping those black market offences that undermined the American war effort, since American capitalism depended on military success, in order to gain control of crucial Asian markets.[9] Immediate easy profit was in this case opposed to long-term interests. On the other hand, violations of the anti-trust laws (involving monopolistic control of certain markets) do not pose a threat to the social structure of American capitalism and can, therefore, be tolerated. The crucial question then that must be asked of white-collar or any other offences is – what effects do these crimes, and public awareness of them, have on the social order? The answer to this question can only be given by examining a specific example of criminal activity in its own particular socio-historical context. The focus should no longer be on the strategies used to avoid prosecution but rather on the *effects* of different kinds of crime. It is then possible to explain why the state wishes to prosecute certain offences and not others.

I wish to concretise these points by critically examining conventional accounts of the development of American capitalism and the related development of anti-trust legislation.[10] The inadequacies of such accounts call for a more sophisticated analysis which entails redefining the nature of American society, both past and present.

2. The Development of Anti-Trust Legislation

Conventional wisdom admits that in the late nineteenth-century when America had a harsh laisser-faire economy, some businessmen, the so-called 'robber barons',[11] tried to make profits at all costs, even if it meant violating the basic principle of the economy. They tried to gain monopoly control of industries by forming 'trusts' – a term applied to an industry if it was effectively controlled by one firm or a working alliance of firms.[12] General opposition to such monopolies, the argument continues, led to the passing of a number of laws to stop them being formed.

> The anti-trust laws are designed to protect competition; they are also designed to protect the institution of free competition as the regulator of the economic system and thereby to protect consumers against arbitrary prices, as well as being designed to protect the institution of democracy against the dangers of great concentration of wealth in the hands of monopolies.[13]

The first of these laws, the Sherman Act, was passed in 1890 at a time of general opposition to the 'robber barons'. It declared:

> Every contract, combination in the form of trust or otherwise, or conspiracy,

in restraint of trade or commerce among the several states, or with foreign nations, is hereby declared to be illegal.[14]

Although the Act seems explicit enough, a great deal still depended on judicial interpretation, and, in fact, the legislation was rarely invoked during the McKinley and Roosevelt presidencies. In 1906 three more acts were passed regulating the meat industry, (Meat Inspection Act); foodstuffs (Pure Food and Drug Act); and the railroads (Hepburn Act). Later, in 1914 during Woodrow Wilson's administration, the Clayton Act and the Federal Trade Commission Act were passed to strengthen the anti-trust legislation. The latter Act provided for the setting up of the Federal Trade Commission. In a period of 25 years a whole new set of laws had been created to regulate the economy, and according to a recent chairman of the Federal Trade Commission this resulted in the growth of economic individualism and the fostering of free and fair competition.[15] Monopoly, in whatever form, was condemned, at least in principle. As a result of popular pressure the free-enterprise system was now protected by law.

Present-day society is thus seen as no longer dominated by the excesses of a laisser-faire economy. Public relations men, the mass media and the school and college textbooks picture it rather as a humane capitalist one.[16] There is now mixed economy where competition is regulated, stability achieved and full employment maintained by government intervention. But the economy is still fundamentally based on the private ownership of wealth. US Steel characterised it as a 'competitive system . . . an acknowledged profit and loss system, the hope of profit being the incentive, and the fear of loss being the spur'.[17] But the large corporations use any advantage which they gain from their size to reduce prices and/or act in a community-conscious way. Overall, 'one needs only to look at the great achievements and standards of living of the American people to see the advantages of our economic system'.[18]

This persuasive picture of the nature and development of American capitalism cannot explain significant features of American society now or earlier in the twentieth century. For instance, in 1918 the Export Trade Act allowed for the *monopolisation by certain firms of key foreign markets*, although this had been explicitly forbidden by the Sherman Act. Moreover, these anti-big-business acts had in many cases been supported *by the businesses they were supposed to regulate*. Thus, the railroads supported the Railroads Regulation Act of 1906[19] and the Chicago slaughterhouse owners supported the Meat Inspection Act of the same year.

These inconsistencies call into question the whole basis of the conventional picture of American society. In contrast to this, I suggest the following model:

1.   The capitalist is committed to profit and growth, which are realised in an exchange, wage-labour, economy.[20] This is not necessarily a laisser-faire economy (it could be a monopoly), and indeed, a disguised monopoly is the ideal.

2.   In order to achieve his goals, the capitalist requires an environment which is predictable, and as much as possible under his control; this is best achieved when

    a.   he has *stability* – when he can control competition and prices (particularly those of raw materials).

    b.   he can *predict* the actions of others – he can control consumers, dominate labour, and effectively influence the government.

    c.   he has *security* – from any kind of movement to limit his power, particularly those that may affect him through the formally democratic institutions.

3.   The action of the large capitalists towards different institutions and groups is *essentially calculative* and will depend upon such factors as their consciousness of what is occurring (as in the case of consumers), on their degree of organisation and strength (e.g. labour), and on the amount of interference that can be expected (e.g. government). The capitalist loyalty to democracy is only provisional.*

---

*This really is the logical conclusion of Max Weber's analysis of capitalist rationality. In his terms, 'A capitalistic action [is] one which rests on the expectation of profit by the utilisation of opportunities for exchange, that is on [*formally*] peaceful chances of profit.' (*The Protestant Ethic and the Spirit of Capitalism*, London: Unwin 1930, p. 17.) The way in which the exchange rate is determined is unspecified, it does not depend on supply and demand but rather on the cost of reproduction of labour-power, which depends in part on union organisation. Weber

Although the form of capitalist organisation may change – as with the present move to large corporate structures – and although the relationship of American capitalism to such things as the world market altered significantly during the period being discussed, it is still comprehensible in terms of this paradigm.

3. Corporations and the Federal Agencies

The attitude of the large corporations to the anti-trust laws developed from hostility in the late nineteenth-century to an active involvement in their administration by 1914.[21] Gordon's comments on anti-business legislation go a long way towards explaining this:

> The state may be pressured either nominally or effectively to prosecute the wealthy if their criminal practices become so egregiously offensive that their victims may move to overthrow the system itself. In those cases, the state may punish individual members of the class in order to protect the interests of the entire class. Latent opposition to the practices of the corporations may be forestalled, to pick several examples, by token public efforts to enact and enforce anti-trust, truth-in-lending, anti-pollution, industrial safety and auto safety legislation. As James Ridgeway has most clearly shown in the case of pollution, however, the gap between the enactment of the statutes and their effective enforcement seems quite cavernous.[22]

In the latter half of the nineteenth century big business attempted to realise its primary goals of profit and growth by gaining control of entire industries. This was to be achieved by the 'trusts', in which all aspects of business, from the supply of raw materials to the sale of goods to the consumers, were brought under monolithic control. By the end of the century

also says that the capitalist has a calculative attitude towards social relationships. However, his life is geared to achieving his major goal of profit. The implication of this is that if there are contradictory claims made on a capitalist's loyalty, and he has the power to do so, he will resolve them in favour of profit. In other words, compared to his pursuit of profit, his other loyalties are merely provisional. This explains how capitalism has successfully developed in pre-democratic countries such as nineteenth-century Britain; how it has coexisted with militaristic and fascist regimes in Japan and Germany; and how at present many of the countries with investments by, or trade with, US business have dictatorial regimes.

there was a Whisky Trust, a Sugar Trust, a Lead Trust, a Cotton Oil Trust, and the controversial Standard Oil. The trusts used any method, legal or illegal, in order to gain, consolidate and maintain their monopolies. By their control of raw materials firms such as Standard Oil bankrupted competitors.[23] Where these methods were not possible, this firm used violence against rivals: in 1887 Standard Oil paid another company's employee to blow up his employer's oil refinery.[24] Violence was also frequently used against organised labour. In one incident gangsters were sent from New York to break a strike of Erie brakemen.[25] Government intervention, if it occurred, invariably aided the employers.

The 'robber barons' were indifferent to the law. One of them, Daniel Drew, stated explicitly that:

> Law is like a cobweb; it's made for flies and smaller kinds of insects, so to speak, but lets the big bumblebees break through. When technicalities of the law stood in my way, I have always been able to brush them aside easy as anything.[26]

But they were to change their attitude to the law in the subsequent twenty years or, more accurately, were to break it less flagrantly.

One reason for this change was fear of radical agitation. There was widespread popular opposition to them and their methods. Political pressure from other businessmen, farmers, workers and consumers made them liable to *unpredictable* court interference, particularly at the local state level. They recognised that this resentment might develop into some kind of socialist movement that would fundamentally transform the social order. Sherman placed strong emphasis on this danger when he argued for his anti-trust legislation.[27]

The Sherman Act did not, however, quiet the popular sentiment, which was particularly strong at the local state level. Prosecutions under state laws against monopolies were frequent. This led the companies and their papers such as the *Railroad Gazette* to agitate for the transfer of these powers to the federal level *where they would be able to effectively control the implementation of Federal regulation of their activity.*[28]

Although there is general belief that the merger movement was widespread in America in the late nineteenth century, and that it was due to the superior efficiency of large-scale business, 'in effect the merger movement was largely restricted to a minority of the dominant American industries, and that for only a few years'.[29] Despite their ruthlessness, their size and the advantages supposedly derived from economies of scale, the merger movement had more or less fizzled out by the end of the nineteenth century.

	average number of firms merging per year	average capital ($ million)[30]
1895-1904	301	691
1905-14	100	221

The merger movement had been given strong stimulus by promoters who benefited from the return of economic prosperity in 1897: it was not inspired by considerations of efficiency. US Steel was capitalised at $1,403 million at the time when maximum efficiency was achieved by plants costing $25 million. The movement was an attempt to achieve effective control of the key industries in America, but due to the expansion of markets and the availability of alternative capital, this control proved elusive.[31]

With the failure of illegal and merger techniques, the larger trusts used two major methods to try and achieve effective domination. In certain key industries acts were passed allowing for governmental regulation of rates and prices, outlawing unfair methods of competition (which usually meant outlawing dangerous small rivals) and sometimes introducing production standards that only the largest firms could afford.[32] The 1906 Meat Inspection Act certainly gained much popular support because of the muck-raking activities of Upton Sinclair, but it also delighted the large meat-packers. It helped them export successfully by fulfilling the high safety standards demanded by the European countries who imported the meat, but it crippled smaller companies. Americans were left with poor quality meat and the working conditions and wages of the workers – Sinclair's major concern – were left unaffected. Governmental regulations provided a means by which monopoly could be achieved against dangerous competitors and without the dangers of popular reactions.

The large corporations also attempted to influence the government. They succeeded with President Theodore Roosevelt. Despite his reputation as a reformer, the few anti-trust prosecutions he initiated had little bite. He preferred the weapon of adverse 'publicity' and formed the Bureau of Corporations with this in mind, but he was confused as to the nature, merits and dangers of big business. He saw them as efficient and inevitable, yet he was concerned about the political and economic power they might yield. He thought that the dangers could be avoided if there were 'good' men in control and if the 'bad' men and the 'bad' trusts were punished. Those who, like US Steel's Judge Gary, gained the President's confidence avoided prosecution. In 1907, Roosevelt approved US Steel's takeover of Tennessee Coal and Iron for $45 million, although a little investigation would have shown that it was worth $180 million and that unfair coercion was used in the sale.[33] Others, like Standard Oil, made a poor impression and became the epitome of the 'bad' trust. Although Roosevelt initiated the investigation of Standard Oil, it was not until 1909, during President Taft's term of office, that it was eventually prosecuted. In 1911 the American Tobacco Company was broken up and 63 other prosecutions were initiated during Taft's presidency (compared with 44 during the eight years of Roosevelt's).

The system of informal détentes had broken down. The corporations became aware of their precarious position in relation to the federal government and at the same time were recognising their vulnerability to prosecution by socialist-controlled state legislatures.[34] President Wilson shared their concern, and during his presidency the legal situation was radically modified. Legislation was passed making regulation a Federal responsibility, and creating agencies responsive to the interests of big business.

The most important of such legislation was the Federal Trades Commission Act of 1914. The provisions of the Bill were formulated by Davies, Head of the Bureau of Corporations, who himself was strongly influenced by prominent corporation lawyers. A presidentially appointed five-man commission was set up with jurisdiction over areas already dealt with by the

Justice Department. They declared:

Unfair methods of competition...unlawful, and the commission was auth-
orised to prevent them from being used. Upon calling a hearing, the
commission could issue 'cease and desist' orders which could be enforced
by Circuit Courts. The commission might also compel the production
of information and utilise the power of subpoena, with penalties for
refusal to co-operate. The commission could gather and issue information
of a more general sort, and advise the Attorney General on correcting
illegal corporate actions.[35]

The precise meaning of this Act was unclear; there was little
direct specification of appropriate penalty or of what constituted
an offence. In practice, these would be defined by those who
administered the Federal Trade Commission, the Inter-State
Commerce Commission and the Anti-Trust Division of the Justice
Department. Of these three, the most significant was the Federal
Trade Commission. In 1916 the first chairman, Hurley, was
very open about how he saw his role:

When I was offered the place, I told the President that all I knew was
business, that I knew nothing about the new laws, nor the old ones
and that I would apply the force that I might have in the interest of
business.[36]

The previous year he had made his intentions quite clear:

We are making an inquiry into the coal industry today with the hope
that we can recommend to Congress some legislation that would allow
them to combine and fix prices.[37]

The large banks were similarly aided by the Federal Reserve
Act of 1913, and even seemingly progressive legislation such
as the Underwood Act of 1913 attacked *small* business by reducing
the tariffs in the markets that it dominated. Thus, an analysis
of the force and meaning of this (and any) legislation must
be clear about what is being prohibited, who is prohibiting
whom, and what sanctions are being applied.

By 1914 the major foundations for the new social order
were well established, big business was consolidating its control
over the major political parties, some of the wind had been
taken out of radical movements because 'something' had been
done, and the legal structure was one that would help rather
than hinder the actions of these powerful men. But their commitment to legality was and is pragmatic, their attitude being

determined by the extent to which it helps them realise their goals on the one hand, and the possible consequences of ignoring the law, on the other.

The history of anti-trust legislation since that period is relatively uneventful. Although there have been amendments to all of the acts, more important has been such legislation as the Wheeler Act of 1938 which deals explicitly with consumer protection. This Act made the Federal Trade Commission responsible for consumer protection and provided a range of sanctions that could be utilised. I will return to this point later.

I have presented an account of the development of the anti-trust laws which suggests that their content and the mode of their implementation have been very different from what one would expect from the conventional accounts of Sutherland, Kintner, etc. In order to understand their importance in American society, I will now examine the number of prosecutions under these laws, who was prosecuted and under what conditions, and then relate these to the frequency of *actionable* practices by corporations. The number of prosecutions will be seen to be so small compared to the degree of violation that the few prosecutions that do take place must have a function other than that of regulating business activity. Such prosecutions, I argue, serve to dramatise an 'imaginary social order' and hence to legitimate the economic structure by a misleading portrayal of its nature. They further appear to vindicate the claim that the state is neutral, in that it seems every group, no matter how powerful, is subject to the will of the majority.

4. The 'Dark Figure' of Corporate Crime

The frequency of prosecutions under the anti-trust laws has been calculated by Hofstadter. He points out that after the demise of the anti-trust movement, the number of prosecutions surprisingly increased.

> During all the years from 1891 to 1938, the government instituted an average of nine cases a year... In 1940, with the Roosevelt-Arnold revitalisation well on its way, the number of cases jumped to 85 – only two less than the number instituted during the entire first two decades of

the Sherman Act. Thereafter, the number of cases, though still fluctuating, stayed at a level considerably higher than that maintained before 1938. In 1962, the anti-trust division employed 300 lawyers and working with a budget of $6,600,000 instituted 92 cases.[38]

Interesting as these figures are, they do not justify Hofstadter's claim that the anti-trust laws are significant regulators of business activity: 92 prosecutions hardly constitute an avalanche, and business activity more than doubled in the period in question. To assess the significance of this number of prosecutions, it is necessary to estimate how widespread is the forbidden activity; only by doing this can one understand the functions fulfilled by particular degrees of enforcement.

Enforcement is undertaken by both the Justice Department and by the Federal Trade Commission, with a great deal of overlapping. The Commission, which has an annual budget of $14 million and a staff of 1,200, has powers to issue 'cease and desist' orders, demand information from firms, and publish what it feels should be made general knowledge; initiate binding actions on companies for contempt; and also alert the Justice Department to infractions which might well lead to prosecution. The Justice Department itself is less actively involved in the regulation than in the Commission, but it has instituted some of the more important prosecutions, such as the prosecutions of the large electrical companies in 1960 after the Tennessee Valley Authority (TVA) had complained of price-fixing.

This latter case is revealing; it shows the conditions under which prosecutions are likely, and it also provides information which can be used to help determine the 'normal' practices in American industry. The TVA announced in 1959 that it had once again received identical secret bids for three contract awards it had advertised to the electrical industry. Further investigation took place, and 'a sampling of TVA records turned up 24 instances of matched or identical bids in just over three years. Some of these bids figured down to a hundredth of a cent.'[39]

Pressure was then brought to bear on the Justice Department which had already been investigating this industry for ten years. It prosecuted the companies: they entered a plea of 'nolo contendere', thereby admitting their guilt but limiting the details of their offences that would be made public. When judgement was given, 29 corporations and 45 individuals were punished. The 29 corporations paid fines *totalling* only $1,787,000. The 45 executives were fined a total of $137,000 and seven served 30-day jail sentences.[40]

It is difficult to know how much illegal excess profits was made by these companies in this particular market. However, some indication of its scale is provided by the amount of money that General Electric paid out in treble-damage suits to companies and governmental agencies who claimed compensation. By 1964, General Electric had paid out $160 million; this meant (because of a treble-damage clause) that it had made at least $53 million excess profits in that market area. But was this atypical? The President of General Electric said it was. He claimed that as early as 1946 employees had been warned against collusion, and that he himself in 1954 had sent out 'Directive Policy 20.5' which reaffirmed this. He defended General Electric by saying that this directive had been issued again in 1958 and 1959, and in fact seemed to view this as a complete legal defence.[41] The convicted employees had a different view. The ex-Vice-President of General Electric claimed that he had been told early in his company career that if he wished to be successful, he should involve himself in such activity. Another employee agreed with Senator Carroll that he had been 'thrown to the wolves to ease the public relations situation . . . that had developed since these indictments'.[42]

Fortunately, there is additional information available which allows a reasoned judgement of the issue. The company directives were probably inspired by pragmatic reasoning rather than by any firm commitment to their content. The 1958 reissue of 'Directive Policy 20.5' occurred at a time when the price fixing agreements in the switchgear and transformer markets had just broken down, thereby allowing for righteous competition. The 1959 Directive was issued at the time when Philadelphia juries were deciding whether there was a *prima facie* case for the prosecution or not. In the months immediately following the plea of 'nolo contendere', identical bids were *still* being made by these companies for TVA contracts. On 14 December 1960, both General Electric and Westinghouse opened identical bids of $1,680,120 for lightning arrestors, on 12 January identical bids of $808·40 were made on current transformers; and on 30 January, five firms, again including General Electric, bid $274·50 for bus type insulators.[43] *It is not possible to explain this systematic continuous behaviour in terms of the 'greed' of a few individuals.* Price-fixing was part of the standard modus operandi of these large firms.

Business in general seemed to view these revelations with little surprise or indignation. The ex-Vice-President of General Electric, within a month of joining another large company, became its President at a salary a little under $74,000. Indignation was rare because this was normal business practice.[44] Once again, such a prosecution by condemning an infraction as illegal and abnormal served to *dramatise an imaginary social order.*

A faith in this unreal world was expressed by the Chairman of the Federal Trade Commission when he attacked the 'Nader's Raiders Report' on his Commission. Although the report deals with the consumer-protection role of this agency rather than its anti-trust work, the Chairman's views inform his practice in both spheres of activity. He wrote:

> The primary difference between the fundamental position of the Nader group and that of myself is that I believe that the American businessman is basically honest and they believe he is basically dishonest, trying consistently to defraud the American consumer. The group contends that American business, particularly the larger corporations selling directly or indirectly to consumers and using extensive advertising, are engaged in what are, or should be, criminal activities and that the officers of these corporations should be sentenced to terms in federal penitentiaries...(whilst successfully using voluntary compliance methods in most cases) with its limited personnel the commission realised that it had to reserve its litigation procedures for use against that small percentage of businessmen in the business community that refused to follow advice.[45]

This statement becomes even more remarkable when one realises that officials of the Federal Trade Commission itself have estimated that in 1968, when robbery netted $55 million, *detectable* business fraud netted in excess of $1 billion, and further that large corporations are knowingly involved in such frauds as those concerning home improvement where Alcoa and Reynolds play an important role.[46]

This attitude to business is consistent with the historical

development of the Federal Trade Commission. The close relationship between the regulators and big business is what one would expect. The interchange of personnel between the large corporations and this agency only underlines the importance of asking of laws, not only what they forbid, but by whom are they administered?[47] The primacy of big business interests is demonstrated by the pattern of enforcement.

The marginal area of textile and fur mislabelling has been vigorously investigated and publicised, allowing for prosecution of mainly Japanese and other foreign businesses, and leading the public to think that these are major areas of abuse.

This 'imaginary social order' is the one mentioned earlier as communicated by public relations men, school texts, etc. The full picture seems to have these elements:

1. The economy is based on private property; there are many shareholders. (Magruder quotes the figure of 25 million.)

2. As a mixed economy, it still has as an essential feature, the pursuit of profit in a competitive market.

3. Large corporations grew naturally because of their efficiency compared to other firms.

4. They maintain their importance because they benefit from economies of scale, and invest most money in research and development.

5. Nevertheless, if they were not efficient, the market would ruthlessly remove them; the market breeds efficiency; competition is central to the system.

6. Ownership and control are separated, allowing for a community-conscious managerial group.

This view is naive and misleading. Baran and Sweezey have shown how large firms actually control prices in an essentially monopolistic way: competition is virtually eliminated by price leadership, and where that does not occur more explicit forms of collusion of the kind already mentioned take place. The theorists of managerial control, such as Mason and Berle, argue that corporations do effectively control their markets. The idea that control *by* the market produces efficiency thus becomes problematic and the legitimation of private enterprise in those terms spurious.

The evidence for a high degree of concentration in industry

is now indisputable. Adolf Berle, writing in 1964, pointed out that:

> Today approximately 50 per cent of American manufacturing – that is everything other than finance and transportation – is held by about 150 corporations reckoned, at least, by asset values. If finance and transportation are included, the total increases. If a rather larger group is taken, the statistics would probably show that about two-thirds of the economically productive assets of the United States, excluding agriculture, are owned by a group of not more than 500 corporations. This is actual asset ownership... But in terms of power, without regard to asset positions, not only do 500 corporations control two-thirds of the non-farm economy but... a still smaller group has the ultimate decision making power.[48]

Not only is the economic power concentrated in a few firms, but these are owned by a small numoer of individuals.

In 1949 the top one per cent of spending units owned more than 75 per cent of marketable stock, and later surveys show that there has been no redistribution of stock ownership since. Top-level management in these large corporations also own a great deal of stock, receiving financial rewards in terms of stock options.[49]

It is evident that a small minority of the American people have a controlling influence on her economy. It may well be true that 'nearly 25,000,000 persons in the United States own shares in American business today',[50] but less than two million of these own most of it. Given American dominance in the world market it is then very possible for crucial economic decisions to be made by this small group.

If corporations are not directly controlled by the market are they at least more efficient because of their size? In one study of firms in industries of above average concentration, it was found that 'concentration by firms in every case but one was greater than required by single plant economies and in more than half of the cases very substantially greater'.[51] Firms are larger than they need be for economies of scale. Large corporations charge far more than is economically necessary for products showing that either they are inefficient or they are making very large profits indeed:

> The Senate Small Business Committee announced that in one contract in 1959 General Electric had charged the navy $82 per unit of carbon blacking, while a smaller company in Hackensack, New Jersey, had charged $15, representing an overcharge of 446 per cent.[52]

What of technological development? Again, research on innovations has shown that large corporations do not necessarily play a leading role.

> In a study of the 60 most important inventions of the recent years, it was found that more than half came from independent inventors, less than half from corporate research and even less from the research done by large corporations.[53]

As usual one can rely on General Electric for a clear statement of the position. T.K.Quinn, a former Vice-President of General Electric, admitted:

> I know of no original product invention, not even electric shavers or heating pads, made by any of the giant laboratories or corporations, with the possible exception of the household garbage grinder... The record of the giants is one of moving in, buying out, and absorbing the smaller creators.[54]

Furthermore, most research today is funded by the Federal Government. The continuing success of the large corporations is due rather to their economic power, by means of which they either take over or intimidate competitors. From the evidence, it is clear that they have a monopolistic control of the economy. Firms either collude illegally to fix prices, or large firms, such as US Steel, dictate prices via price leadership.[55]

On closer analysis then, the commonsense picture of the nature of the American economy, and of the relationship between large corporations and the government, proves to be illusory and misleading. The degree of concentration and the extent of their control of the market means that the large corporations continually violate the anti-trust laws. For, although price leadership is not itself illegal, it could not even occur if there were not an 'unreasonable' concentration of market power.[56] Nader's analysis of the position of General Motors suggested a

> ...test of unreasonable market power in terms of its size and the sources of that power, and its growth through mergers and acquisitions of more than 100 companies, including Olds Motor Works, Cadillac Motor Company, and Fisher Body. The Standard Oil, Alcoa and Dupont cases, amongst others, are relevant authoritative interpretations of the anti-trust laws for application to the General Motors situation.[57]

Finally, such analyses of industry are supported by one of the Federal Trade Commission's own statements:

The Federal Trade Commission has estimated that if highly concentrated industries were broken up by the anti-trust laws into more competitive companies so that the four largest firms in any industry would not control more than 40 per cent of that industry, prices would fall by 25 per cent or more.[58]

The above analysis of the nature and extent of anti-trust violations required an appreciation of the way in which capitalists' commitment to profit and growth, and their calculative attitude to economic, political and social relationships, made them willing to act illegally when it was in their best interest. Only by using a similar framework can one make sense of the incidence and patterning of their violations of the labour laws administered by the National Labor Relations Board.

5. Corporatism and Labour as a Factor of Production

Under capitalism employees are regarded primarily as producers and as the consumers of at least some of the goods manufactured. Laws concerning 'fair labour practices' have been supported in so far as they helped towards efficient production, when they have not done so they have been ignored.

Despite the reluctance to use the law against corporations there have been many recorded violations of the labour laws by businessmen. Sutherland found that, in the period 1890-1949, 44 out of 70 large corporations had been prosecuted for unfair labour practices.[59] But rather than detail these incidents, the specific content of the labour laws and who effectively controls their implementation,[60] I wish to focus on the relationship between capital and labour. This will provide a better basis for understanding both the criminal acts and the legal response.

According to the capitalist world view, labour is merely a factor of production, and like all such factors, it is desirable that it should be calculable and controllable. If labour does not accept such an interpretation of itself certain problems may be created which the ruling class will then solve pragmatically, according to their perception of the realities of the situation. Whatever solutions are chosen, they maintain a belief that the interests of labour are essentially the same as those of capital. *Corporatist presuppositions are fundamental to a capitalist view of these relationships.*

Such corporatism expresses itself in two major ways: if the unions are weak, then each individual firm is seen as an entity and all members of it are expected to belong to one organisation – the company union; if the unions are relatively strong, then attempts are made to form joint organisations on a national level such that capital, labour and the government can work together, but to achieve *capitalist* goals. Whichever model predominates at a particular time, it will undoubtedly be corporatist in emphasis. The mode of co-option, either individualistic or via the independent union structures, will depend pragmatically (but not necessarily cynically) on the corporate élite's perception of the situation.

There has been an enduring belief in the corporate nature of society; in 1901, the *Banker's Magazine'* wrote:

The growth of corporations and of combinations tends to strengthen the forces which seek to control the machinery of the government and the laws on behalf of special interests... That they are not entirely controlled by these interests, is due to the fact that business organisation has not reached full perfection... Every professional man, as well as all who pursue every other mode of livelihood, will be affiliated by the strongest ties to one or other of the consolidated industries. Every legislator and every executive officer will belong to the same head. Forms of government may not be changed, but they will be employed under the direction of the real rulers... The direction of the industrial and producing force would enlarge independence in some directions while it might restrict it in others. Wisely conducted, every citizen might, according to his merit and ability, attain higher prizes in life than is possible at the present time.[61]

In the 1950s this view was still retained in its essentials, but modified to the extent that unions, rather than individuals, would be co-opted. In the new order, self-governing but *non-democratic* corporations would be the basic units. These would include everybody and labour unions could play a consultative role, provided that they abandoned the right to strike. In this neo-corporate feudal order, the central government would be little more than *primus inter pares* because: 'You don't have such a function [coping with economic, political and military problems] over to the government – the national government. You hand over this function to a new kind of corporation.'[62]

Adolf Berle, who had been chairman of President Kennedy's Task Force on Latin American Policy and Special Assistant to the Secretary of State, clarified how this system would be legitimated. It was pointless, he argued, to use normal democratic procedures by consulting the people as a whole, because this provided only superficial public opinion; rather, the system would be legitimate if it were acceptable to the public consensus, based upon

> the conclusions of careful university professors, the reasoned opinion of specialists, the statements of responsible journalists, and at times the solid pronouncements of respected politicians...the real tribunal to which the American system is finally accountable.[63]

This corporatism expressed itself in the efforts of business to involve the unions in organisations like the National Civic Federation (NCF), founded in 1900,[64] which was supported by business and liberal political leaders and publicly advocated the right to unionisation. It attracted conservative trade-unionists, and significantly because unionism was strong at the time, gave them support against those radicals who stressed the irreconcilable nature of the conflict of interest between labour and capital. The NCF continued to be important into the 1930s and succeeded in attracting Samuel Gompers and many of his followers. Under Franklin D.Roosevelt and the New Deal, the proclaimed unity of interest of State, Labour and Capital was given institutional expression in the National Recovery Administration.

Although 'fair labour' laws had been passed (paralleled by the corporations' exemption from prosecution under the anti-trust laws), by 1934 many of the conservative trade-unionists were disillusioned with this co-operative arrangement. They argued that the unions were losing many rights and had little real say in any important decisions. The rank and file were discontented with the contradiction between the publicly declared policy of the corporations on unionisation, their support of 'fair labour' laws and how they acted in their own industries. As early as 1919, the Inter-Church World Movement had condemned the hypocrisy of US Steel for preaching welfare capitalism at NCF meetings, but practising the worst tyranny against its own workers, using intimidation and blacklists and discharging union men.

The large corporations violated National Labor Relations Board regulations based on laws passed at times when it was necessary to recognise, institutionalise and incorporate trade unions via their conservative leadership. For, despite the laws, attempts were made to establish in practice the primacy of the individual contractual relationship between the corporation and the employee. Laws lose their binding power when they are no longer based on the realities of power, and the punishment then meted out for violations is relatively light. These laws were used as part of an overall strategy for pre-empting the radical potential of an increasingly powerful trade-union movement – they suggested that America was really a democracy since everyone, rich and poor alike, was subject to legal constraint. But when the danger was neutralised, when the unions were coopted, the laws could be safely ignored. It was for this reason that corporation executives were willing to break the laws that they themselves had advocated.

6. The International Dimension

The contradiction between the actual workings of the social order and the ideological picture of the nature of capitalist society has been laid bare by analysing the reasons for the demonstrable lack of fit between legal prescription and actual behaviour. In doing so it has become clear that knowledge of the laws is a poor guide to how the corporation will act and a poor guide to how the state will react. It is necessary to go beyond the commonsense (and legal) understanding of the legal institutions. It is necessary to ask not only *why the laws have been passed* (and whether they are implemented) but *why some laws have not been passed*. This is particularly relevant when the organisation of institutions seems to violate their declared purpose. Thus the oligopolistic organisation of the press in Britain seems to be at variance with the notion of an open market of information and opinions, yet there is a voluntary body, the Press Council, that is meant to oversee the situation. On closer analysis this proves to be under the control of the major newspaper publishers (even the lay members of the council are chosen by the professionals) and was probably constituted to pre-empt the formation of a body under public control.[65]

The foreign relations of America are justified to her people in terms of her commitment to the 'free world' – a world of democracy and free enterprise. The incompatibility between this picture and the real relationship to other countries rarely becomes fully visible because few laws concerning the regulation of international commerce and intercourse exist to highlight them. Moreover, although capitalism is itself an *international* system, dominated for the last twenty years by the USA, people still think in national terms. (This includes criminologists, who, even when they talk about social control are bound by commonsense nation-state units of analysis.)

The large corporations, however, have not confined their activities to America itself. Since the First World War, they have been involved in the administration and direction of American foreign policy. Their confidence in the competitive advantages held by American business, their need for new markets and the importance to them of raw materials that were either naturally available abroad, or could be more cheaply produced in 'underdeveloped' countries, explain this involvement. Since the Second World War, the importance of military expenditure to the revenues of the largest corporations has strengthened their interest even more. The government (mainly through defence spending), and foreign buyers now account for 20 to 40 per cent of the total demand for the products of all the major industries, with the exception of agriculture.[66] The corporate rich are involved in foreign policy decisions of the American government, in order to protect and develop their overseas interests, and also in their capacity as virtually equal partner with the military. That their interests have been by far the most important in shaping American foreign policy is now extremely well documented. The change of attitude towards Russia after the Second World War can no longer be explained in terms of Russia's aggression,[67] but rather must be understood as due in large part to the economic consequences of the spread of communism. As a former American Ambassador to the Soviet Union put it: 'Every time Russia extends its power over another area or state, the United States and Great Britain lose another market.'[68]

When, after the efforts of McCarthy and the 'cold war' doctrine, radicalism in any country, as in America, could be dismissed as a Russian plot, American intervention to protect business interests was readily legitimated. Since these large corporations are heavily involved in other countries, it is very relevant to determine whether they act criminally in this situation too. This is a complex problem. It has already been established in this essay that one can only understand their illegal acts by redefining these as actions which, at a particular time, were the most effective way to help realise the dominant goals of profit and growth. I have shown that from the point of view of the corporation there is no intrinsic difference between a legal and an illegal act.

International business activity is supposedly governed by conventions and laws and is legitimated to the peoples of the world in those terms. But there has been little development of either international or national law to cope with the emergence of the large American-based monopolies. These companies achieve control of their foreign markets and sources of raw materials by methods that continually violate international norms and national laws: information about this is systematically denied to the American people by governmental and corporate misrepresentation.

In the underdeveloped countries, similar attempts are made to mislead the indigenous peoples who are said to have an irrational distrust of American business. One writer suggested that the 'image problems of American corporations abroad' would be solved by the general adoption of an advertising programme designed by an agency for one of its clients. Nine features of a desired image were outlined, four of which were:

1. The company is an important tax contributor to the national government.

2. The company puts the broad national welfare above immediate profits.

3. The company does not interfere in any way with national political decisions.

4. The company takes a sincere interest in community problems.[69]

It is interesting to apply this model to a not atypical country, Guatemala. In 1950, Jacob Arbenz, having received 267,000 of the 350,000 votes cast, became President of his country. He continued and developed social reforms started by his predecessor, Juan José Arrevalo. One such reform involved distributing idle land to poor peasants. The American-owned United Fruit Co. was informed that it would have to surrender some of its land. It was offered compensation based on the value set on the property in 1952 for tax purposes 'by the owner himself'. Although United Fruit objected, it was expropriated. In 1954 a group of Guatemalan exiles, led by Colonel Carlos Castillo Armas, invaded Guatemala from Honduras and Arbenz fled into exile.

America still claims that Arbenz's government had been taken over by communists (despite all the evidence to the contrary). It does not mention its own connection with Armas,[70] who was trained at the US Command and General Staff School at Fort Leavenworth, Texas, or that the whole operation was financed, armed and organised by the CIA. The Secretary of State at the time, John Foster Dulles, was a major stockholder and long-time corporation counsellor of the United Fruit Co.[71]

This example is revealing for a number of reasons. Clearly both the United States government and the United Fruit Co. colluded in *illegally* undermining a legitimate government. The willingness to sacrifice democracy when it interfered with corporate action underlines the tenuous and provisional nature of their commitment to democratic institutions. If those who espouse socialist ideas are elected, they can be removed relatively easily because of the vast military might of America compared to that of poorly organised local people. The need to take such action is often avoided by actively funding undemocratic regimes which would otherwise be replaced by the inhabitants of those countries. 'One quarter of outright US grants in the period 1946-61 went to five countries – Turkey, Greece, South Korea, South Vietnam and Formosa – all right wing dictatorships opposed to social change, and with the exception of Formosa, all hopelessly backward economically.'[7][2]

There can be no theoretical justification for confining one's analysis to those occasions when regimes are illegally undermined. They must be understood as only one strategy developed to control and guarantee the supply of raw materials.

7. Summary

This essay has attempted to show that to understand the 'crime' problem in America one must relate four things:

1. The publicly declared 'crime problem'.

2. The 'ideological' portrayal of American society as being a *democratic* free-enterprise system, wherein the majority rationally control the legislature and the government. This is the *'imaginary social order'*.

3. A more accurate picture of the distribution and mode of criminal activity in the American social structure – using as criteria of significance those adopted in the first point above.

4. A picture of American society based on a radical and more sophisticated analysis of the relationship between the capitalist class and the state, the nature of the economic order, and the problems posed by insulating this against democratic attack. The focus here is on the 'real social order'. (By contrasting 'ideological' and 'real' I am not implying that we can interpret social reality other than by theorising about it, merely that I have proposed an analysis that not only provides a better explanation of what is going on than does the 'ideological' one, but also explains the functions of this inaccurate portrayal.)

When examining specific kinds of criminal acts and the actual societal response to them, I have shown that the major determinant of police actions is the relationship between the criminal activity and the 'real social order'. Actions that pose a real threat to this must be controlled, e.g. embezzlement or lower-class attacks on private property. I have also suggested that by police action the state stabilises the system by mystifying the people. The occasional implementation of laws that attack the rich seemingly gives content to the claim that the state is neutral and controlled by the people. Furthermore, in focusing on and incarcerating lower-class criminals, the major individualistic ideologies are upheld and the potential for developing radical political movements based in the lower-class is at least partially neutralised.

Although I initially started this analysis of corporate crimes within a very legalistic framework, I have progressively moved further away from the confines of positive criminology. Once criminal activity is viewed as one amongst other strategies used by corporations, then one is forced to analyse the overall social structure within which they act. This not only leads to posing the questions as to why laws are implemented in this way and why laws are not passed, but also to recognizing that the international nature of the capitalist system is reflected neither in the system of regulation nor in most theorising about it. Thus, in analysing 'crimes of corporations' we are ultimately led to ask fundamental questions about the nature of American and the world's 'free enterprise system'.

Notes

1. *The Wisdom of Spiro T. Agnew*, New York: Ballantine Books 1969, p.40.
2. J. Edgar Hoover, 'The Faith of Free Men' in Richard D. Knudten (ed.), *Criminological Controversies*, New York: Appleton-Century-Crofts 1968, p.10. Since that time there is no evidence of appreciable change in the FBI's views.
3. The President's Commission on Law Enforcement and Administration of Justice, 'Crime and Victims in a Free Society', 1967, excerpted in Carl A. Bersani (ed.), *Crime and Delinquency*, London: Macmillan 1970, pp.5-7.
4. Quoted in Murray Kempton, 'Crime Does Not Pay', *New York Review of Books*, 11 September 1969.
5. The President's Commission on Law Enforcement and Administration of Justice, *op.cit.*, p.8.
6. Gabriel Kolko. *Wealth and Power in America*, New York: Praeger 1962, pp.20-22. See also Robert J. Lampman, 'The Share of Top Wealth Holders in National Wealth 1922-1956', in Maurice Zeitlin (ed.), *American Society Inc.*, Chicago: Markham 1970.
7. See the general discussion of the confines of traditional criminological thought in Herman and Julia Schwendinger, 'Defenders of Order or Guardians of Human Rights?', *Issues in Criminology*, Vol. 5, no. 2, Summer 1970.
8. David M. Gordon, 'Class and the Economics of Crime', *Review of Radical Political Economics*, Vol. 3, no. 5, Summer 1971, pp.64-67. Things are not always so straightforward as is evident from the politicisation of prisons in America and the emergence from that system of such thinkers as Malcolm X, Eldridge

Cleaver and George Jackson; cf. *The Autobiography of Malcolm X*, Harmondsworth: Penguin 1968; Eldridge Cleaver, *Soul on Ice*, London: Cape 1969; George Jackson, *Soledad Brother: The Prison Letters of George Jackson*, Harmondsworth: Penguin 1971.

9. cf. Marshall B. Clinard, 'Criminological Theories of Violations of Wartime Regulations', *American Sociological Review*, 11 June 1946, pp.258-70, reprinted in Gilbert Geis, *op.cit.*, pp.71-87; Anthony Sampson, *Sovereign State: The Secret History of ITT*, London: Hodder & Stoughton 1973. On the Second World War see John Bagguley, 'The World War and the Cold War', in David Horowitz (ed.), *Containment and Revolution*, London: Anthony Blond 1967, pp.76-124.

10. See the accounts presented by Sutherland in the various works quoted and Edwin W. Kintner, *An Anti-Trust Primer*, New York: Macmillan 1964; and Richard Quinney, *The Social Reality of Crime*, Boston: Little, Brown 1970, pp.73-77.

11. For an account of business activity in this period of American history see below and Matthew Josephson, *The Robber Barons*, London: Eyre & Spottiswoode 1962.

12. See Gabriel Kolko, *The Triumph of Conservatism*, Chicago: Quadrangle Books 1963, p.17.

13. Gilbert Geis, *op.cit.*, p.354.

14. Edwin W. Kintner, *op.cit.*, p.266.

15. *ibid.*, p.15.

16. The following picture is a composite, relatively consistent one communicated by these diverse sources. The texts I consulted are Californian schools' standard texts: economics courses use James N. Dodd, *Applied Economics*, Cincinatti: South Western 1945; compulsory civics courses use William A. Clenaghen, *Magruder's American Government*, Boston: Allyn & Bacon 1969, 52nd ed.

17. From the *Corporation Report* of US Steel in 1958, quoted in J.K. Galbraith, 'The Corporation', in Jerome R. Skolnick, *Crisis in American Institutions*, Boston: Little, Brown 1970.

18. William A. Clenaghen, *op.cit.*, p.16.

19. Gabriel Kolko, *Railroads and Regulations 1877-1916*, Princeton: Princeton University Press 1965, pp.144-51.

20. A more accurate characterisation of a capitalist economy requires a discussion of the 'capitalist mode of production'; see Karl Marx, *Capital*, Vol.1, Moscow: Progress Publishers 1965.

21. For this analysis I have relied mainly on the following works: Gabriel Kolko, *op.cit.*, 1963; Gabriel Kolko, *op.cit.*, 1965; Martin J. Sklar, 'Woodrow Wilson and the Political Economy of Modern United States Liberalism', James Weinstein, 'Gompers and the New Liberalism 1900-1909', Ronald Radosh, 'The Corporate Ideology of American Labor Leaders from Gompers to Hillman', all in James Weinstein and David W. Eakins (eds.), *For a New America*, New York: Random House 1970; Richard Hofstadter, 'What Happened to the Anti-Trust Movement?', in *The Paranoid Style in American Politics*, New York: Vintage Books 1967.

22. David M. Gordon, *op.cit.*, p.62.

23. Matthew Josephson, *op.cit.*, pp.379-80, 109-20.

24. *ibid.*, p.269.

25. *ibid.*, pp.372, 364.

26. Gilbert Geis, *op.cit.*, p.48.

27. Richard Hofstadter, *op.cit.*, 1967, p.197.

28. Gabriel Kolko, *op.cit.*, 1965, p.143.

29. Gabriel Kolko, *op.cit.*, 1965, p.19.

30. *ibid.*, pp.10-19.

31. In the telephone industry, for example, the competition from the independents broke AT&T's monopolistic position, which it had held 1885-1894. By 1910 the telephone rates had been forced down by this competition, and the dividends paid out by AT&T had sharply declined, whereas those paid out by many of the smaller companies were still healthy. Gabriel Kolko, *op.cit.*, 1965, pp.47-50.

32. In Britain the passage of the regulations concerning working conditions in factories can be viewed similarly. Large-scale industry pragmatically supported such regulation because it was bad economic sense to train and discipline workers who soon after they had reached their peak of efficiency might be rendered unproductive through an industrial accident. On this issue there was a conflict of interest between the large and small proprietors. Marx commented that 'if the Factory Acts, owing to their compulsory provisions, indirectly hasten on the conversion of small workshops into factories, thus indirectly attacking the proprietory rights of the smaller capitalists, and assuring a monopoly to the great ones, so, if it were made obligatory to provide the proper space for each workman in every workshop, thousands of small employers would, at one fell swoop, be expropriated directly!' (Karl Marx, *Capital*, Vol.1, Moscow: Progress Publishers 1965, p.482.)

As we know, factory legislation was passed and a special agency was set up to deal with its implementation. In a recent study of this law-enforcing agency, W.G.Carson made the following comment about the officials' attitude to violators: 'It was when a firm's previous history was interpreted as an indication of its unsatisfactory attitudes rather than its adverse economic position or otherwise extenuating circumstances that severe enforcement was likely to ensue.' (W.G.Carson, 'White Collar Crime and the Enforcement of Factory Legislation', *British Journal of Criminology*, Vol.10, 1970, reprinted in W.G.Carson and Paul Wiles, *Crime and Delinquency in Britain*, London, Martin Robertson 1971, p.202.)

Carson argues later in his article that there was 'no conscious bias in the administration of justice'. It may be true that there was no conscious bias but that does not mean that there was no bias. Although larger *firms* may have received no more consideration than smaller *firms*, to treat the possibility of maiming or killing another human being as less important than making profits is surely a clear example of bias. Not one for which some individual can be selectively blamed but one upon which the whole society exists, i.e., the need for profit is primary and other things must be sacrificed if they interfere unduly with its realisation.

33. Gabriel Kolko, *op.cit.*, 1965, p.116.

34. For a documentation of the number of socialists in local government see Edwin Lemert, *Social Pathology*, New York: McGraw-Hill 1951, p.177.

35. Gabriel Kolko, *op.cit.*, 1965, p.267.

36. *ibid.*, p.275.

37. *ibid.*, p.270.

38. Richard Hofstadter, *op.cit.*, p.194

39. James Herling, *The Great Price Conspiracy*, Washington: R.B.Luce 1962, p.62.

40. Gilbert Geis, *op.cit.*, pp.105-6.

41. James Herling, *op.cit.*, p.13.

42. Gilbert Geis, *op.cit.*, p.111.

43. Jerry de Munh, 'GE: Profile of a Corporation', *Dissent*, July-August 1967, p.504.

44. The *illegal* excess of American Telephone and Telegraph Company's current revenues over the maximum supposedly in force (the rate of return is set by the Federal Communications Commission) is approximately $169 million p.a. P.Lassell & L.Ross, 'Nixon's Economic Melodrama', *New York Review of Books*, 23 September 1971.

45. Chairman Paul Rand Dixon in Edward F.Cox, Robert C.Fellmeth, John E.Schulz, *Nader's Raiders Report on The Federal Trade Commission*, New York: Grove Press 1970, p.184.

46. *ibid.*, p.56.

47. *ibid.*, p.122.

48. Quoted in Jerome Skolnick, *Crisis in American Institutions*, Boston: Little, Brown 1970, p.123.

49. For further documentation of this see Gabriel Kolko, *op.cit.*, (1962), and William Domhoff, *Who Rules America;* see Paul Baran and Paul Sweezey, *Monopoly Capital*, Harmondsworth: Penguin 1966.

50. William A.Clenaghen, *Magruder's American Government*, Boston: Allyn & Bacon 1969, p.16.

51. See Walter Adams, 'Competition, Monopoly and Planning', in M.Zeitlin (ed.), *American Society Inc.*, Chicago: Markham 1970.

52. Jerry de Munh, *op.cit.*, p. 593.

53. Walter Adams, *op.cit.*

54. Paul Baran and Paul Sweezey, *op.cit.*, p.49.

55. *ibid.*, Ch.3.

56. See Edwin R.Dew (ed.), *The Economics of Anti-Trust*, Englewood Cliffs: Prentice-Hall 1968.

57. Ralph Nader, 'GM & The Auto Industry, the Threat of Corporate Collectivism', in J.Solnick, *op.cit.*, p.141.

58. Quoted in Ralph Nader, 'A Citizen's Guide to the American Economy', *New York Review of Books*, 2 September 1971, p.15.

59. Edwin Sutherland, *White Collar Crime*, New York: Holt Rinehart & Winston 1949, and Jerry de Munh, *op.cit.*, pp.509-12.

60. For this see Loren Baritz, *The Servants of Power*, New York: John Wiley 1960, pp.158-66.

61. Quoted in Gabriel Kolko, *op.cit.*, 1963, p.162.

62. Quoted in Hal Draper, 'Neo Corporatists and Neo Reformers', in *New Politics*, Vol.1, no.1, 1960.

63. *ibid.*, p.96.

64. The following account is constructed from the material presented in the articles by James Weinstein, Philip S.Foner and Ronald Radosh in James Weinstein and David W.Eakins (eds.), *For a New America*, New York: Random House 1970.

65. This is virtually admitted in Harold Levy's book on the Press Council *(The Press Council*, London: Macmillan 1967), a publication with a foreword by its Chairman, Lord Devlin (later replaced by Lord Pearce). The Press Council has become a more independent voice, with increasing numbers of lay members, and it is now frequently contacted by members of the government and official bodies. It was criticised by the 1962 Royal Commission on the Press and also by the 1972 Younger Commission on Privacy. Nevertheless, it is often very protective of vested interests e.g. in its evidence to the Maud Commission on Defamation where it opposed legal aid in such cases despite the strictures of writers like D.N.Pritt in his *The Substance of the Law*, London : Lawrence & Wishart, 1972, ch.2) and has consistently avoided confronting the real dangers to the 'freedom of the press' from monopoly whilst approving of the restrictive provisions in the Industrial Relations Act (see *Press and the People*, 1972).

66. Harry Magdoff, *Economic Aspects of US Imperialism*, Monthly Review Press : New York, p.16.

67. Whatever Russia's intention, she was in no position to engage in aggression, since during the Second World War she had lost 20 million dead; one third of her territory was devastated; and she had lost two-thirds of her industrial base. David Horowitz, *op.cit.*, 1969.

68. *ibid.*, p.71.

69. Helen Dinerman, 'Image Problems of American Corporations Abroad', in John W. Riley (ed.), *The Corporation and Its Publics*, New York : John Wiley 1963, p.157.

70. See for example the account of these events in *The US Department of State Facts Book of the Countries of the World*, New York : Crown Publishers 1970, p.270.

71. David Horowitz, *op.cit.*, 1965, pp.163-86.

72. *ibid.*, p.195.

3.

Organised Crime
in Historical Context

1. Introduction

In Part 3, I examine the literature about organised crime and its relationship to American society. I have selected the most socially significant, the most scholarly and the most comprehensive analyses of the phenomenon so that, by using a marxist approach, even such relatively rigorous accounts can be seen to be conceptually inadequate, to have an often dubious factual basis and to ignore important dimensions of the problem. I hope, through the substantive discussion that follows, to vindicate the claims made earlier that marxism transcends other approaches to social phenomena.

The gangster is a twentieth-century figure that symbolises a side of America which, although it is unique to that culture, has much resonance in other western countries – the enormous international box office receipts of *The Godfather* testify to this. Many see him as one of the few figures able to make his own space in the world by smashing through the routines and constraints of everyday life in a bureaucratic industrial society. Needless to say such romanticism is not normally shared by law-enforcement officers. The late J. Edgar Hoover characterised the problem of organised crime in terms of a dangerous, national conspiracy to undermine American institutions. Relying to a large extent on the testimony of Joseph Valachi, a New York gangster who appeared in 1963 before the second McClelland Committee, Hoover claimed that:

> La Cosa Nostra is the largest organisation of the criminal underworld in this country, very closely organised and strictly disciplined. They have committed almost every crime under the sun...
> La Cosa Nostra is a criminal fraternity whose membership is Italian either by birth or national origin, and it has been found to control major racket activities in many of our larger metropolitan areas, often working in concert with criminals representing other ethnic backgrounds. It operates on a nationwide basis, with international implications, and until recent years it carried on its activities with almost complete secrecy. It functions as a criminal cartel, adhering to its own body of 'law', 'justice' and, in so doing, thwarts and usurps the authority of legally constituted bodies.[1]

This statement was a departure from Hoover's previous position on the Mafia, for prior to the early sixties its existence had always been denied by the FBI. They did not accept the evidence presented to the Kefauver Commission in 1951 by Harry Anslinger, the then Director of the Bureau of Narcotics. They continued to be sceptical after the 'underworld convention' of Italian-American gangsters was discovered in the Appalachians in 1957.

The change in the FBI's attitudes has been associated with quite dramatic changes in legislation and police practice. A Labor-Management Reporting and Disclosure Act was passed in 1959 to clean up the unions and the Organised Crime Control Act was passed in 1970. Such legislative innovation is explicable neither in terms of public conern nor of startling new revelations, for the Kefauver Committee had received as much publicity as the McClelland Committee, yet Kefauver's proposals were never implemented.

The laws passed and the activities of the law-enforcement agencies since the war bear witness to an unevenness in the state's response to organised crime that requires explanation. Furthermore, there seems little connection between the legal innovations requested and granted and the effective elimination of organised crime. Ex-Attorney General Ramsay Clarke has pointed out that electronic surveillance, the extensive use of which has been justified by the needs of the 'war against crime', has never been used to procure convictions of known racketeers. (This is not too surprising when one reads the trivia in tape transcripts of conversations such as those of the New York gangster 'Sam the Plumber' Cavalcante.[2]) The most successful police work has been undertaken by federal strike forces that have visited cities and pooled the available information (gathered without electronic surveillance) and then presented a case to a special Grand Jury. Clarke claims that, as a result, federal indictments associated with organised crime jumped from 19 in 1964 to 1,166 in 1968.[3] Furthermore, as I will show later, the laws mentioned above were not primarily designed to fight organised crime but rather to combat radicalism, and indeed, most electronic surveillance (and many of the other activities of the FBI) have been used against those defined as *politically* dangerous.[4]

The plan of Part 3 is as follows. It begins by examining critically the view that organised crime is controlled by a national Italian-dominated Cosa Nostra and then goes on to deal with

114

another view which considers it an 'American way of life'. These must be replaced by an alternative view which stresses the significance of 'grass roots' organisation, of corruption and of ruling-class tolerance. This idea, of *the underworld as servant*, is the basic theme of this essay.

An examination of Chicago during the Prohibition years will show that Capone was removed when he seriously interfered with corporate interests. A survey of labour racketeering and the state's response to its perpetration from the 1920s through to the late 1950s tells the same tale. It has been encouraged, ignored or repressed in direct relation to its utility to the American ruling class.

In the previous part of this book and in the article, 'Crime, Corporations and the American Social Order'[5], I have argued that a major failure of criminology has been its neglect of the international dimension of both criminal behaviour and social control mechanisms. Similarly, it is in the context of her economic and political struggles with other nations that the complexity of the American state's relationship to organised crime becomes manifest. Well-known gangsters were used both inside America and in Italy to help further her aims during the Second World War. Since then in Sicily, France, South Vietnam and Laos American governmental agencies, notably the Central Intelligence Agency, have directly sponsored local organised crime to further American foreign policy. Since in all of these countries groups of American protégés have become involved in the trade supplying heroin to the expanding American market, there has been, ironically, an important conflict of interest between the CIA and the Bureau of Narcotics! However, the international links go even deeper. Americans had an important stake in the rackets – particularly gambling and prostitution – during Batista's corrupt rule in pre-revolutionary Cuba. The recent Watergate scandal in America revealed interesting evidence of connections between the anti-Castro Cubans, organised crime and Nixon's Republican machine. This makes even more ironic the spectacle of a 'law and order' President forced to resign because of his unethical and illegal conduct. High-minded commitment to 'freedom from communism' is seen to be once more tied to unsavoury personal interests.

Finally, section 7 again looks at ruling-class opposition to organised crime. An examination of the content of the legislation passed in recent years shows that this opposition is very selective and that much of the time the major target is organised radicalism – particularly those willing to use violent methods as were the Weathermen – rather than syndicated crime or those who make a living from criminal enterprise.

This is not meant to be an exhaustive treatment of the subject of organised crime in America. Consequently, where there already exist adequate analyses of certain aspects of the subject, I have used but have tried to avoid unnecessarily duplicating them; the two most important examples of this are Mary McIntosh's *The Growth of Racketeering* (1973), and Joe Albini's *The American Mafia: Genesis of a Legend* (1971). There is a dearth of good empirical material, since the questions that flow from a marxist analysis are not the same as from any of the major traditions of criminology or deviancy theory in America. The writings on Prohibition Chicago, for instance, are very deficient in describing the class structure and dynamics of that particular urban conglomerate; as a result such questions as the relationship between the ruling class and the rest of society have had to be treated somewhat speculatively. Accounts of the development of the labour movement during the forties are still few and are primarily sectarian tracts, whether of the left or the right. The rewriting of earlier American history already undertaken by Weinstein, Kolko, Lynd, O'Connor and their comrades which stresses the role of the state and the dialectic between repression and mass action, trade-union participation and socialist consciousness has not yet reached this decade. Once again I have been forced to be rather assertive instead of relying confidently on scholarly work. These difficulties are at present insuperable but hopefully suggest new lines of socialist research.

2. The Myth of a National Mafia

To do justice to the official account of the Mafia/Cosa Nostra I will supplement J. Edgar Hoover's statements with the work of sociologist Donald Cressey. In his book *Theft of the Nation* (1969) he presents a picture much the same as the report of the President's Commission on Law Enforcement and the Administration of Justice (he was one of their consultants). He suggests that since the end of the last century, when Italian and Sicilian immigrants came to the New World in large numbers, there has been a Mafia of some kind in America, although it is unclear whether or not this is the same one as that found in Sicily. Until Prohibition the American Mafia was not particularly important except to those living inside the Italian 'urban villages'. The large-scale demand for an illicit commodity, alcohol, made its provision a profitable venture. But it also led to extensive internecine strife among the gangs involved and this required resolution. Such a service was provided by the Mafia. After widespread gang wars in 1930 and 1931 Salvatore Marranzano called a meeting in New York. Mobster Joseph Valachi attended and provides this account of what occurred:

> He, Marranzano, was speaking in Italian, and he said, 'Now it's going to be different'. In the new set-up he was going to be the *Capo di tutti Capi*, meaning the 'Boss of all Bosses'. He said that from here on we were going to be divided up into new families. Each family would have a boss and an underboss. Beneath them there would also be lieutenants, or caporegimes. To us regular members, which were soldiers, he said, 'You will each be assigned to a lieutenant. When you learn who he is, you will meet all the other men in your crew'.[6]

Sometime in the next few years (Cressey equivocates on when) an exclusively Italian national organisation, the Cosa Nostra, was established, based on this model. 'The Nationwide criminal cartel and confederation' founded then is the 'Italian organisation that controls all but an insignificant proportion of the organised crime in the United States'.[7] It is seen as being both a government and a business enterprise, with a complex structure and clearly articulated roles. It has a national commission whose membership is drawn from the Cosa Nostra, although not all are represented. Its major function is to allocate territory and to settle disputes.

117

There is also, in some parts of the country, another level, a council, but its purpose is obscure. The most important unit is the 'family' of which there are 24 or so in America. They are organisationally identical and have distinct territories. Each has a boss ('don'), an underboss ('sottocapi'), and a counselor ('consigliere') and a buffer, then lieutenants ('caporegime'), section chiefs and finally soldiers. To summarise, organised crime is centrally and bureaucratically controlled by an Italian-American organisation.[8]

It is necessary in assessing this analysis to be clear what one means by organised crime. The kind of phenomenon that Cressey and others are talking about is best described as syndicated crime, which 'differs from other types of organised crime primarily because it provides goods and/or services that are illegal, yet for which there is a demand by certain segments of society'.[9] Bearing this in mind, it seems that Cressey's picture is misconceived. An examination of the history of America in the last century makes clear that no one ethnic group has ever exclusively dominated syndicated crime. 'In many cities, particularly in the South and on the West Coast, the mob and gambling fraternity consisted of many other groups, and often, predominantly, of native white Protestants.'[10]

Furthermore, different gangs from the same ethnic groups do not necessarily unite against other ethnic gangs; in Chicago, for example, O'Banion's Irish gang allied with a Sicilian gang, the 'Terrible Gennas', against the Torrio-Capone organisation.[11] Crime syndicates are often jointly controlled by criminals from different ethnic backgrounds as can be seen from Valachi's account of New York, Bell's analysis of the waterfront, Turkus's and Feder's description of *Murder Inc.*, and Poston's account of the numbers racket.[12] Even detailed analyses of syndicates which are controlled exclusively by Italian-Americans, such as Ianni's New York family,[13] do not reveal an organisation of the kind described by Cressey. Thus to argue that the Cosa Nostra is the national organisational base of syndicated crime is to force the evidence. Albini provides the most damning critique of Cressey's organisational chart, showing the many contradictions in that picture. Many families have different structures, the roles are not clearly defined and the evidence has been gathered from pre-edited transcripts (not original tapes) where there is already a high degree of interpretation. Commenting on the actual chart he says: 'Even the Boy Scouts of America have a far more complex structure than this.' The National Commission also poses problems for Cressey's analysis since Turkus provides accounts of meetings in New York in 1934 when Johnny Torrio from Chicago tried to set up a national organisation of both Italian and American gangsters.[14] Cressey rejects the evidence for this although it is sounder than much he uses himself.

The high proportion of Italian-Americans known to be associated with syndicated crime can be explained without invoking the notion of a Cosa Nostra. Bell points out that, like other immigrant groups, they were initially marginal to the socio-economic and political structure.[15] The employment and business opportunities available to them were initially limited. In such a situation, involvement in crime was understandable and research such as that of Glaser suggests that even today many criminals engage in crime only when they are unemployed.[16] This explains why the ethnic succession among gangsters has tended to follow the immigrant waves: American, German, Bohemian, Polish, Irish, Jewish and then Italian. With the expansion of the American economy some of the previous immigrants had been able to gain footholds in legitimate business. The majority of course were integrated as wage earners: Irishmen obtained lucrative civil contracts through their control of the political machine in New York, German Jews entered banking and merchandising and some of the later Jewish immigrants the garment trade. These legitimate roads to wealth were spoken for by the time the Italians arrived so the entrepreneurially minded made good use of the new opportunities created by Prohibition for syndicated crime. After Prohibition, attempts were continuously being made to move into legitimate businesses but opportunities were still limited.[17] It was therefore logical for them to use their wealth and know-how in other criminal activities; for example, the Capone organisation moved into gambling. There is thus a historical/structural explanation of Italian involvement in crime without invoking notions of a national or international criminal conspiracy.

I have argued that Hoover's and Cressey's picture of an

Italian-controlled criminal conspiracy is a myth, although it is possible that Italian-American fraternal organisations exist. Members of such 'mafias', on the evidence of tape transcripts, seem to engage in some rather trivial activities. Murray Kempton in the *New York Review of Books* quoted and commented rather drily on a phone call by one of Sam De Cavalcante's lieutenants:

> 'Sam, I came to see you yesterday', Riggi says, 'because I felt that, as an amico nos and a caporegime, I'm not getting the respect I should from Joe Sferra.' – Sferra's regime was the Elizabeth Hod Carrier's Local: his affront was not relieving Riggi's father from carrying bricks and finding him a lighter assignment.[18]

The 'Cosa Nostra' can in no way explain the extent, the persistence, or the importance of organised crime in America. No such entity is required in a society dominated by the market ethic where there is a large consumer demand for illegal commodities – alcohol, prostitutes, drugs, gambling; a political system which has successfully excluded even social-democratic parties, leaving politics as little more than an arena for squabbles over the distribution of spoils between rival factions of the ruling class and with a high degree of decentralisation facilitating the corruption of local politicians and police; and a ruling class which is not usually threatened by such crime (whatever the public rhetoric on the subject). At the local level:

> Political corruption has been considered functional to the business community in offering protection against aggressive competition, speed in finalising contracts with government, and freedom from cumbersome codes and regulations.[19]

To put it somewhat differently, entrenched business interests can with minimum visibility guarantee excess profits and ignore safety considerations, as well as ecological and other socially beneficial constraints.[20] At the national level the same freedom is acquired for corporations by their control of the agencies meant to regulate their activities for the common good. Similarly, established racketeers may try to control new members of their fraternity, but the structural context of the supply and demand for illegal commodities is determined by the overall legal and political system; in a real sense organised crime is a 'grass roots' phenomenon.

There has been a long tradition in America of explaining

away behaviour which is against the interests of ruling-class groups as un-American – as the result of impurities, the result of immigration. Thus many Prohibitionists saw drink as an immigrant vice, and alcoholism as both an index and a source of racial degeneracy. 'We are going to have purer blood as the poison of alcohol becomes eliminated', said William Jennings Bryan, 'we are going to have a stronger race because of prohibition.'[21] Despite the strong indigenous socialist tradition,[22] bolshevism, anarchism and other socialist creeds were viewed as foreign in origin; in the twenties, besides the trial of Sacco and Vanzetti, many radicals were deported under the anti-alien laws.[23] Kefauver in his report on organised crime advocated stricter immigration laws.[24] The justification provided for repressive action in section two of the Internal Security Act of 1950 including the following two paragraphs:

> 13. There are, under our present immigration laws, numerous aliens who have been found to be deportable, many of whom are in the subversive, criminal or immoral classes, who are free to roam the country at will without supervision or control.
> 14. One device for infiltration by communists is by procuring naturalisation for disloyal aliens who use their citizenship as a badge for admission into the fabric of our society.[25]

The official view that organised crime, like radical movements, is controlled by a fraternity whose traditions are 'un-American' and whose loyalties are not to the nation but to an international organisation based in a foreign country explains it culturally rather than structurally. The focus for law enforcement and public concern has become the Italian-American community rather than the political and economic system.[26] As a result the racketeering connections of many politicians – such as Johnson and Nixon[27] – are less likely to be investigated. Repressive laws are thereby justified and it is quite certain that chasing such phantoms will not eliminate syndicated crime.

3. Syndicated Crime and Political Influence

A more interesting view than the 'conspiracy theory' is

that put forward by Daniel Bell, who sees crime as 'an American way of life'. He argues that political and economic marginality has led the most recent immigrants at any time to crime; that for the Italians this provided the only road to wealth since legitimate businesses were monopolised by other ethnic groups; and that their sojourn with crime was only temporary until they could invest in legitimate business. Crime was 'one of the queer ladders of social mobility in American life'. Money made in this way also provided a means by which the Italian community could bring influence to bear on the local political machines:

> ... that the urban machines, largely Democratic, have financed their heavy campaign costs in this fashion rather than having to turn to the 'moneyed interests' explains in some part why these machines were able, in part, to support the New and Fair Deals without suffering the pressures they might have been subjected to had their source of money supply been the business groups.[28]

Even in the violent years of industrial relations when gangsters were used by business this was matched by the unions' actions.

> At one time, employers in the garment trades hired Legs Diamond and his sluggers to break strikes, and the Communists, then in control of the Cloakmakers Union, hired one Little Augie to protect the pickets and beat up the scabs; only later did both sides learn that Legs Diamond and Little Augie were working for the same man, Rothstein.[29]

There is no doubt that Bell has achieved a superb integration of very diverse empirical material with a sophisticated, if somewhat cynical, analysis of the development of twentieth-century American society. Certain of his assumptions, however, lead him to ignore crucial aspects of the phenomena under study. He treats the socially mobile as a relatively undifferentiated group, he misunderstands the nature of such phenomena as the New Deal and above all he accepts a pluralistic model of the distribution of power in society.

Although it is true that some of each immigrant wave into America have made themselves business careers, the majority have become wage-earners of one kind or another. There were often sharp divisions in the immigrant communities between those who had a desire to progress in an individualistic way and those who were more committed to collective action. Many

122

of these, through their foreign language federations, were active in the socialist movement in America.[30] This was equally true of the Italian immigrants and there were many Italian socialist papers, with strong working class support.[31] There were serious divisions in the Italian community and there was so much fear of working-class anti-fascism that in 1926, when Mussolini's goodwill ambassador, Commander Pinedo, landed on Lake Michigan, Capone was one of the welcoming committee – to quell any riotous anti-Fascisti.[32] The very term 'Italian community' is an ideological one in that it presupposes a common interest.

Although it is true that for those who were interested in playing the game the Italian gangster's gifts to party treasuries meant that Italians would not be simply ignored by the municipal authorities, it was for the protection of the racketeering and business interests that local ethnic support was sought. The business and racketeering nexus was best served when their customers thought themselves of some account to the local parties. (Capone donated $280,000 to Big Bill Thompson's 1926 mayoralty campaign in Chicago[33]). More recently:

> Alexander Heard, in his book on campaign finances, estimates that organised crime currently pays for fifteen per cent of campaign expenditures at state and local levels. In 1952 that would have been some $16 million – ten times the contribution of organised labor.[34]

Impressive as these figures are, they do not show that organised crime controls local government, but rather that local politics is influenced by it *within limits clearly demarcated by monopoly capital*. Campaign donations are part of the enormous payoffs required for crime syndicates to operate at all. Bearing this in mind it becomes evident that there have been wild exaggerations about syndicated crime's *net* income and also about its influence. Cressey points out that from the $7 billion allegedly made by the syndicates from gambling 'must be deducted the costs of doing business, such as wages, rent, bribery, and arrangements'.[35] Lundbergh has carefully examined the evidence and has concluded:

> While it is no doubt true that people like Costello have accumulated a nest egg of dimensions that might be envied by the common man I doubt that it is very great in the terms under discussion. If Costello

or any other underworld character as of 1965 had a net worth of more than $5 million it would be surprising. No available evidence shows great underworld wealth unless Wall Street is located in the underworld.[36]

Organised crime's investment in legitimate businesses has not been in large-scale manufacture, where there is a very high rate of return, but rather in the more marginal, less profitable service industries such as car haulage, garbage disposal, catering, etc.[37]

The fortunes and influence of organised crime have been limited because the consolidation by the large corporations of their control of the commanding heights of the economy during the first three decades of this century made it extremely difficult for those with limited capital (even if legitimately acquired) to join their ranks. Furthermore, the political dominance by the corporations over the Federal government and also at local level limited other influences. Contrary to Bell's assertions this was also true of the New Deal. Roosevelt's goal was 'to guarantee the survival of private enterprise by guaranteeing conditions under which it can work'.[38] The American polity was not 'up for grabs' – it was already spoken for. Lundbergh reviews the relationship between gangsters and local politics as follows:

> What actually almost always happens is that an established group in business and/or politics having decided what the prospects are, looks about for a strong-arm man. If he can't be found locally he is imported, as Costello was imported into New Orleans to run slot machines, as Johnny Torrio and Capone, Brooklyn men, were imported into Chicago to dominate vice in general and as Harry Bennett was brought to Detroit by Ford.[39]

In other words one must see the underworld as servant. There is no better place to put this view to the test than Prohibition Chicago.

4. The Underworld as Servant: Chicago

Capone's domination of Chicago is legendary. Kobler begins his recent biography with an account of Capone's ability to decide whether or not there should be a clean election in 1928. Allsop sees part of his task to explain 'the genesis of this eventual domination of a city by a criminal dictator . . . whose authority extended, through the State of Illinois and beyond'.[40] This occurred in part because of the subservience of powerful aldermen such as Kenna and Coughlin to Capone and Torrio.[41] Eventually,

> As the vicious criminal elements and their political counterparts became more strongly organised, government was growing more and more disorganised, until it virtually fell apart and capitulated to a ruthless and defiant underworld.[42]

This account of the Prohibition years in Chicago is quite inadequate. It fails to explain why Capone, for all his power, had no choice in 1927 but to obey the Chief of Police's instructions that he should leave Chicago so as not to embarrass the city's mayor Big Bill Thompson in his bid for the Republican presidential candidacy.[43] Nor does it explain Capone's fall from power and eventual imprisonment in 1932. In order to understand the events in Chicago it is necessary first to look at Prohibition itself.

The coming of National Prohibition in 1920, when the Volstead Act came into force, was the successful culmination of many years of agitation. There had been Prohibition candidates for the presidency at most elections from 1884 to 1916, but it was through their influence in the two major parties in the super-patriotic conditions of the First World War that the Prohibitionists finally succeeded. They linked drink with alien influence, racial degeneracy and bolshevism.[44] At the same time they gained the support of the majority of manufacturers. Big business supported Prohibition because it channelled reform sentiment away from economic questions to an ideologically opaque contest between 'village America' and 'urban America'; because dry sentiment and the business ethic of hard work, efficiency, wealth and self-help stemmed from the same Puritan roots – many drys supported manufacturers' efforts to keep down wages because this limited the money available for drink; finally because drinking was seen to interfere with production both through the resulting absenteeism and from inefficient work.[45]

The Volstead Act – the legislative instrument for putting into effect the Eighteenth Amendment to the Constitution – forbade the manufacture or importing of liquor. It did not forbid its purchase nor was the purchaser liable for conspiracy.

Thus the poor who drank and socialised in bars were liable to find their meeting places padlocked whereas the rich carried on entertaining at home from the abundant cellars they had stocked between the ratification of the Eighteenth Amendment and the passing of the Act or from liquor supplied at only the bootlegger's peril. National Prohibition, like other philanthropic movements such as the 'Child Savers', grew out of the rural middle class's paternalistic belief that they had the right to interfere in the supposedly disorganised lives of the urban working class.[46] Like these other movements it was only effective when it had the support of capital. However, in the case of drink such support was far from solid and was only gained by diluting the Act, making it virtually unenforceable and then, because of Congress's ambivalence, providing an inefficient and under-financed Prohibition Bureau.

Chicago was a wet city. Very few of its citizens supported Prohibition, although the working-class immigrants were its strongest opponents. Gangsters were already busy in the city running prostitution and some were brought in by big business for use in the class war – Al Capone had 'helped' settle a newspaper strike. Rival factions of the local political parties used the gangsters to settle disputes, and by the early 1920s a 'perceptible pattern of bold collaboration between politics, business and gangsters was becoming apparent'.[47]

In Chicago local capitalists were at best ambivalent about Prohibition and it had little direct effect on their everyday lives. Some chose to make money from it. Johnny Torrio was in partnership with 'the youngest of four brothers who were rich brewers before the Prohibition . . . The brewer knew the methods of modern business and applied them to syndicated beer-running. Torrio knew the gangsters and recruited them.'[48] There was a more general involvement with gangsters when labour racketeering became important in the late 1920s. In 1928 Capone is thought to have made $10 million of his $100 million (gross) from the 'protection' of small businesses and union corruption. It is hardly surprising that Capone, as an example of the freest 'free enterprise', should be ideologically an ideal partner. Claud Cockburn reports the following conversation with him:

'Listen', he said, 'don't get the idea I'm one of those goddam radicals.

126

Don't get the idea I'm knocking the American system...'

'...This American system of ours', he shouted, 'call it Americanism, call it Capitalism, call it whatever you like, gives to each and every one of us a great opportunity, if we only seize it with both hands and make the most of it.'[49]

In other cities like San Francisco clear alliances were made:

[The] underworld element, professional politicians and corporations, these all supported the District Attorney, Flickert, who had refused to clean up the red light district, when he was opposed by a respectable reform group with union and IWW backing.[50]

Despite local corruption in Chicago and elsewhere, law-enforcement agencies had found no difficulty in indicting, convicting and often deporting socialists and anarchists. The American socialist movement of the time was recognised as a very real threat by the ruling class.[51] By 1919 the Socialist Party reached a membership of 109,000, only a few thousand below its 1912 total, and Chicago was one of the strongholds of the movement. At that time, Chicago was one of the sites chosen to give a legal gloss to the persecution of the Wobblies, who had been harassed, misrepresented and illegally intimidated by press, vigilante mobs and police.[52] In the 1920s the Farmer-Labor Party had extensive trade union support in the city and in the thirties the unemployed workers movement was to be strong there.[53] The use of Chicago's police for political ends was infamous. The late John Williamson, a communist victim of the Smith Act, made this comment:

Chicago's factories spilled their dirt and soot over miles of flat land inhabited by their workers. The stockyards and railroads added their stench, and the polluted river cut through its center. The South Side housed the nation's second largest concentration of urban negroes; near the stockyards was virtually a Polish city. Here the first strike for an eight hour day took place; here the Haymarket martyrs met their death, here was the founding place of the Social Democratic Party, led by Eugene Debs, the Industrial Workers of the World and the Communist Party ...Nowhere was police terror so bad as in Chicago during those years. Corrupt to the core and in alliance with the gangsters, the police arrested hundreds of workers at meetings, demonstrations and strikes and beat them into insensibility in the local police stations.[54]

Although there had been the alliances between gangsters and capital, if racketeering was seen to be against capitalist interests it was soon attacked. This can be seen in the early twenties when in the case of 'labour racketeering' the opportunity was also taken to undermine union organisation. In 1921-2 the Chicago building trades were controlled by an alliance of corrupt union leaders and the suppliers of building materials. This proved expensive to the construction companies and promoters were unwilling to go ahead with building. At the same time militant trade unionists were opposing attempts to cut their wages and impose an 'open shop', as had been recommended during one dispute by an arbitrator, Judge Landis, who was against corruption but was also anti-union.

> To meet this situation of union opposition and to make the Chicago construction industry 100 per cent Landis there was formed the Citizens' Committee to enforce the Landis award – the first organised and large-scale intervention in the affairs of Chicago building trades by parties outside the industry. The Committee was organised under the auspices of the Association of Commerce, with the support of many architects and bankers, and its membership was made up of persons having no direct interest in the construction industry, however much interest some of them may have had in the issue of the open versus the closed shop.[55]

This was a clear case of the interests of particular capitalists being subordinated to that of the class as a whole. It also provides the key to Capone's later downfall.

By 1926 some business leaders, lawyers and academics had become sufficiently concerned with the breakdown of law and order to form the Illinois Association for Criminal Justice, which commissioned the *Illinois Crime Survey* (in print in 1929). In addition, the Chicago Crime Commission, founded in 1919, became ever more active and citizens' groups were formed, the most famous of these being the Chicago Association of Commerce Sub-Committee for the Prevention and Punishment of Crime. This was known as the 'secret six' because the chairman, the President of the Chamber of Commerce, Colonel Randolph, refused to reveal the names of the five other businessmen on the Committee.[56]

Many businessmen had begun to feel that City Hall could no longer be relied upon to provide the 'rational legal' form of administration that they required to run their businesses. Chicago's judges were corrupt, her administration was inefficient, civic contracts were awarded to the highest briber; the infrastructure was starting to break down. The true magnitude of the city's crisis became clear in 1930 when it was found to be $300 million in debt. Mr Silas Strawn, a civic finance expert who headed a Rescue Committee formed under an emergency measure to save the city from ruin reported:

> Mismanagement by Mayor Big Bill Thompson and his friends, and lethargy on the part of the public, have reduced Chicago to bankruptcy, the chaotic plight of the public services is now revealed. Unless citizens put money in the till on a large scale, hospitals will shut, inmates of lunatic asylums will be left without food, heat or light, prisons will be unable to house their tenants and the police and fire brigade will have to be disbanded . . .[57]

This situation prompted a deputation of 'prominent' Chicago citizens, led by newspaper publisher Frank Knox, to appeal to President Hoover to intervene. He was sympathetic, possibly in part because of the links between local businessmen and the Republican Party: in 1928, the Chicago civil reformer Julius Rosenwald of Sears Roebuck had contributed $50,000 to Hoover's campaign fund.[58] In 1929 federal proceedings were started against Capone for income tax evasion and Elliot Ness and his Department of Justice Raiders started to destroy his breweries. Capone tried to reach an accommodating detente with the authorities – including big business interests – but failed,[59] and three years later, much to his surprise, he was given a ten-year sentence. There was no doubt who really controlled Chicago. As one of Capone's contemporaries said to Allsop:

> Capone and the others really believed that they were running the city, but I don't believe they were. They were the executives and the technicians. The city was being run by the politicians and by City Hall, and the big bosses weren't interested if the gangsters killed each other, providing they kept delivering the money.[60]

Although Prohibition had been supported initially by much of big business, its unintended consequences – and Chicago was only an extreme example – made many change their mind. The depression was an important factor, for, as Andrew Sinclair wrote:

> This lawlessness, spawned by prohibition, now threatened to spread with mass unemployment, and shake the roots of society. The same employers who had supported the Eighteenth Amendment a decade earlier to benefit themselves and their workers now advocated repeal to protect themselves from their workers. They hoped that legal beer would relieve some of

the social tensions of the time and lessen class hatred...There were other reasons for the manufacturers to change over to the side of repeal. The first was that prohibition seemed to have lost them more than it had gained. The deficiency in government revenue from the liquor tax had been made up by a tax on the incomes of the wealthy and of corporations. The restoration of these incomes would be an incentive to business in the depression. Moreover, the labour unions still existed outside the saloons, and were strengthened when their members attended sober labour meetings. The failure of federal law enforcement showed that private laws of the major companies against drinking by employees, which were widely used before prohibition was sufficient to prevent industrial accidents; indeed it was preferable for the workers, if drink they must, to drink good beer rather than bad hooch. Also the increased consumer market promised by prohibition had not materialised.[61]

The publication in 1931 of the Wickersham Report on the enforcement of Prohibition provided extensive documentation of its impracticability and harmful effects and in 1932, the year after Roosevelt's election to the presidency, it was repealed.

I have analysed Capone's career in Chicago because I think that it shows clearly how much is ignored by most conventional accounts. There is no doubt that Capone was a powerful man, but there is equally no doubt that when he started to interfere with the interests of corporate capital, the limitations of his power became clear. This point is still valid today in Chicago. No matter how corrupt its local politics, civic decisions always take into account the interests of the ruling class.[62] In law enforcement this is clear too. In 1968, during the Chicago Democratic Convention, those so brutally attacked and beaten on Mayor Daley's orders were explicitly opposing the power of the corporations. Law enforcement has always been taken very seriously when its goal has been the suppression of radicals.

Yet opponents of syndicated crime often write as if the state does not have sufficient power to cope with it. Kefauver recommended a strengthening of the immigration laws despite the extensive powers already available and despite their frequent use against Italian socialists.[63] Cressey categorically states: 'Organised Crime, in all its varieties, flourished in the United States because the criminal law cannot effectively be used to attack organisations.'[64] Although Cressey expresses concern over legislation that might undermine traditional freedom, his failure to examine American history critically makes such statements mystifying since America has one way or another always denied such 'freedoms' to socialists.

Having dealt here with syndicated crime I will now turn to the analysis of labour racketeering. It must be treated in some depth because it is here that conventional accounts of organised crime fail most miserably.

5. Ruling Class Sponsorship of Syndicated Crime

Industrial Racketeering

In the 1920s, in Chicago, New York and elsewhere, many gangsters turned to industrial racketeering as a fruitful source of income. Al Capone, Arnold Rothstein, Little Augie, Louis Buchalter and a myriad of others had been introduced into labour relations as strike-breakers. They soon offered their services as insurance against upsets of any kind, from the unions, from competition or from bombing.[65] This usually involved businesses joining some trade association and/or negotiating contracts with mobster-controlled unions. Although some of the businessmen were far from happy about these arrangements, the cost of protection was usually passed on to customers in higher prices.

> In Chicago racketeering involved most consumer goods and services with a consequent rise in prices. The Employers Association of Chicago estimated the annual cost to consumers at $130,000,000 or about $45 per inhabitant...Towards the end of 1928 the State Attorney's office compiled a list of ninety-one Chicago unions and associations that had fallen under racketeer rule.[66]

Similarly in New York: 'By the early thirties, Louis Lepke dominated a widely assorted number of industries including bakery and pastry drivers, milliners, garment workers, leather workers, motion-picture operators and fur truckers.'[67] Most of these were service or small-scale manufacturing industries. Daniel Bell has suggested an explanation for this:

> Industrial racketeering...performs the function – at a high price – which other agencies cannot do, of stabilising a chaotic market and establishing an order and structure in the industry; industrial racketeering can exist

131

> in a specific type of economic market. It does not exist in steel, auto, chemical, rubber etc., where a few giant firms acting in oligopolistic fashion, establish an ordered price structure in the industry. It has existed in small-unit size, highly competitive local product markets, such as trucking, garment, baking, cleaning and dyeing, where no single force other than the industrial racketeer was strong enough to stabilise the industry. This was especially true in the 1920s when industrial racketeering flourished. In the early 1930s legalised price fixing by the New Deal, through the NRA, undercut the role of the industrial racketeer. What had hitherto been a quasi-economic but necessary function now became outright and unnecessary extortion. And in the garment area (dominated by Lepke and Gurrah Jacob Shapiro), in the restaurant field, and in similar industries infested with industrial racketeers, the employers and the union appealed to government for help.[68]

Bell qualifies this assessment admitting that the New York docks were exceptional in that racketeer control persisted there at least into the fifties (when he was writing). This was because they still fulfilled a useful economic function, the maintenance of an abundant supply of compliant labour available for the irregular loads coming into the harbour. His treatment of this exception will be examined below.

But first I wish to deal with his more general statements within the socio-historical context of America in the thirties and forties. Whilst he is accurate on certain details, his account overall is so partial as to be quite misleading. There is little doubt that as soon as gangsters were no longer of any use to businessmen efforts were made to eliminate them. It is also accurate to point to their regulative function in 'cut throat' competitive conditions. However, it is not true that the New Deal tended to eliminate labour racketeering or that gangsters were not used by the large corporations. Ex-bootlegger Roger Touhy points out that with the end of Prohibition in sight (it was finally repealed in 1935) many gangsters looked longingly at the lucrative union funds because:

> In the late 20s and early 30s the biggest and most solvent treasuries in the world were the labor unions. Some of the old-time labor stakes didn't trust banks. They packed the union's cash away in safe-deposit boxes or invested in US Government bonds. The top American Federation of Labor unions in the Chicago area had about $10,000,000 in their treasuries.'[69]

Getting control of unions provided an easy, safe way of making money. Some years later Dan Sullivan, Operating Director of the Miami Crime Commission, was told how this was done by another gangster who had switched to that field of operations.

> First of all, when you have a check-off system, you have a fool-proof system of collections. It doesn't cost you anything to operate. Secondly, if you run into one of these insurance companies or welfare outfits you don't pay any money out and you take it all in. And thirdly you have no inspection on the local, county, state or federal levy. So your funds are not audited.[70]

Bell claims that such corruption was no longer 'functional' to employers because Roosevelt's National Recovery Administration allowed for legal price-fixing: gangster-dominated employers' associations were no longer required to stabilise industries. However, as Touhy's comments show, industrial racketeering was still prevalent during the New Deal and, as I will show below, not only in the service industries. Why this was so can only be understood by looking at the New Deal itself.

For Bell, as for other corporate liberals,

> What the New Deal did was to *legitimate* the idea of *group* rights, and the claim of groups, as groups, rather than individuals, for government support. Thus unions won the right to bargain collectively and through the union shop, to enforce a group decision over individuals; the aged won pensions, the farmers gained subsidies; the veterans received benefits; the minority groups received legal protections. None of these items, in themselves, were unique. Together they added up to an extraordinary social change. Similarly, the government has always had some role in directing the economy. But the permanently enlarged role, dictated on the one hand by the necessity to maintain full employment, and on the other, by the expanded military establishments, created a vastly different set of powers in Washington than ever before in our history.[71]

Such a view which sees America as being a society of different interest groups exercising countervailing power against each other refereed by a neutral state, albeit one that tends to develop its own interests, is inaccurate. As Tony Woodiwiss has shown, the New Deal was a part of the process by which monopoly capitalism achieved hegemonic domination over American society.[72] There was never any doubt of Roosevelt's commitment to capitalism, but in order to save it from itself he was forced to give it some rather unpalatable medicine.[73]

Roosevelt came to power three years after the Great Crash promising a New Deal which would produce 'a true concert of interests'.[74] This was to be achieved through various bodies known by their initials such as the AAA, the CCC, the FERA, the TVA, PWA and the NRA (National Recovery Administration). It is important to realise that: 'In essence the NRA embodied the conception of many business men that recovery was to be sought through systematic monopolisation, high prices and low production.'[75] One of the provisions of the National Recovery Act, Section 7a, stated that 'employees shall have the right to organise and bargain collectively through representatives of their own choosing and shall be free from the interference, restraint or coercion of employers...'[76] This concession helped win the support for Roosevelt of many trade unionists and initially encouraged many workers to form union locals. But the Act did not ban individual bargaining, company unions or the open shop and the NRA (nicknamed the National Run Around) administrators supported employers in their opposition to working-class militancy.

After the whole NRA was declared unconstitutional in 1935 the President approved the Wagner Act which made Clause 7a more of a reality in order to gain the trade unionists' support. At the same time, as Radosh has argued, certain fractions of the ruling class, particularly corporate capital, recognised that by doing so they could contain working-class militancy – both by limiting its political content and by making its expression predictable.[77] As mass producers they were very conscious of the need for a mass market, and with governmental approval of their monopolistic practices they would be able to pay high wages and still make a good profit. They felt it imperative that the worker 'desire a larger share in the mental and spiritual satisfaction in the property from his daily job much more than a *larger share in the management of the enterprise which furnishes that job.*'[78] [emphasis added]

Overall, 'the New Deal's recognition of potentially antagonistic social groups served a conservative integrating purpose'.[79] This is perhaps the fundamental criticism of the corporate liberal position. The idea of countervailing power in American life fails to explain the historical movement of American society both at home and abroad, because, whatever groups exist, whatever elites there are, 'The men at the top must heed the basic law of our society; the need to expand corporate profit.'[80]

Ideally, then, for employers during Roosevelt's administration company unions were best; failing that came unions which eschewed fundamental questions concerning the organisation of the economy and particularly the organisation of individual enterprises. Although the American working class compared to the British was neither as extensively unionised nor as generally politically self-conscious about the class nature of society and industrial organisation, the socialist organisations, rank-and-file militancy, the Wobblies and the various regional general strikes underlined a dangerous radical potential. One way to cope with the NRA and Wagner legislation was to allow unionisation but to keep it as right-wing as possible. Whereas gangsters had long been used to stop any unionisation, they were now also used to try to emasculate any locals that were set up. They would set up 'paper locals' (local branches only in name, with no control by their rank-and-file members) and negotiate 'sweet-heart' contracts.

The relationship between the Chicago Restaurant Association and the syndicate-manipulated unions since the thirties is a good example of this.

> It was an ideal shakedown racket. There was little book-keeping involved, only names and dues were important, not animated members agitating for union benefits, welfare, meetings, elections or any other kind of legitimate union practises. It was strictly a paper organisation. Meanwhile, the association members were pushing syndicate beer, liquor, meats and produce and were utilising its myriad services; laundry, dry cleaning, garbage disposal, vending machines, juke boxes and buying its fixtures and appliances. The association members contributed to a 'voluntary fund' – aside from its regular membership dues – for use when labor troubles arose, which happened with increasing regularity…It was a classic 'sweetheart' arrangement, for the restauranteers were still coming out ahead by paying below-scale wages, the lowest in most instances in the country. There was something in it for everybody but the workers.[81]

Again, it was after the repeal of Prohibition that mobsters Willie Bioff and Frank Nitto (the enforcer) moved into the movie industry. In 1934 their man, George E.Browne, became President of the AFL union, the International Alliance of Theatrical Stage Employees. Soon on the East Coast 'the wages of union members were slashed and stagehands were laid off'.[82]

Then they moved to Hollywood, but the contract that they wanted this time was not too sweet. The movie companies had to pay $75,000 a year indefinitely and got very little benefit from their association with the racketeers; so, following the typical pattern, Browne, Bioff, Nitto and the other members involved soon fell foul of the law. [83]

Although I have provided some evidence to show that labour racketeering was alive and well during the thirties, the examples I have given are still primarily in the marginal areas of employment, in service rather than in the central manufacturing industries. But this gives a misleading impression of its importance, because even when racketeers operate in such fields as car delivery this may be because they have rendered 'services' to the major manufacturers. I have already mentioned that racket-dominated unions do not, as a rule, negotiate tough wage contracts. In the heavy industries they have had the additional function of stopping the growth of a strong, militant, socialist trade union movement. The concessions made to labour in the 1930s made only too possible the democratic election of socilaists to union positions and the spread of socialist ideas amongst the working class, particularly those in such large-scale enterprises. United Steel battled against unionisation as such; [84] other employers reluctantly accepted the unions and then attempted to control their policies by having either AFL unions (committed to Gompers business unionism) and/or corrupt unions. The best documented case of this is in the centre of America's manufacturing industry, Detroit.

Detroit: Opposition and Co-option

The Kefauver Commission found that syndicate men Anthony D'Anna and Joe Adonis had been given monopolistic franchises in Detroit and New Jersey for the haul-away business at Ford. This was part payment for service rendered to Harry Bennett, who had been labour boss at Ford's Detroit plant. When Michael D. Whitty followed through the story, partially revealed in Kefauver's book, he uncovered a plot which demonstrated the utter ruthlessness of corporate capitalism: gangsters were to be used to gain control of the unions in all auto work in Detroit.

The struggles to organise the autoworkers in America were

some of the most heroic in American union history. The large corporations involved used every weapon in the employers' vast armoury to stop unionisation. Company spies were used; in 1934 General Motors alone spent $839,000 on detective work, and Chrysler gave $211,000 to the Corporation Auxiliaries Co. which provided spies and stool pigeons.[85] General Motors was also a member of the National Metal Trades Association which, besides supplying labour and scabs, helped set up company unions and worked with the Justice Department and Naval and Army Intelligence. Workers sympathetic to unionism were either laid off or terrorised. Gangsters were used, particularly by Fords; General Motors

> used the forces of notorious Black Legion, a Dupont financed terror group that beat, tarred and feathered and murdered active trade unionists. General Motors foremen were actually seen donning black robes inside the plant in preparation for a Black Legion raid.[86]

Although the AFL had made half-hearted attempts to organise the autoworkers, it was not until 1936 with the UAW-CIO that any headway was made. Once the union started to recruit members it became unstoppable and use was made of the sit-down strategy which was sweeping America at the time. At the end of December, the 'Great Flint Sit-Down Strike' began. As a result in February 1937 General Motors recognised the UAW as the sole bargaining agent and agreed to no reprisals. General Motors was organised.[87]

This did not necessarily mean that other auto companies would also capitulate. Ford held out until 1940, using its own private army to oppose unionisation. This was the 3,000 men in Harry Bennett's Service Department. He employed ex-pugs, policemen who had been fired from their jobs, gangsters and men released from prisons: men, like 'Legs' Laman who had a record as a gunrunner, kidnapper and squealer and who, after six years in prison, was paroled in the care of the Ford Motor Co. Another was Chester La Mare, a powerful Detroit gang leader who in 1929 was granted the fruit and vegetable concession worth $100,000 a year, at River Rouge. Still another was Sam Cuva, who was gaoled for shooting his mother-in-law.[88] From 1937 to 1940, when attempts were made to organise the company, the Service Department beat up many union organisers including Walter Reuther. However, in 1940 after union and NLRB pressure, the Ford Motor Co. gave in.

Harry Bennett agreed to a union shop, dues check-off, grievance machinery, seniority, time and a half for overtime, premium pay for night workers, and two hours pay for employees called in but not given work.[89]

There has been much speculation about why Ford capitulated.

Was it, as some observers felt, a move dictated by the simple business considerations that it might be cheaper to work with the union than to fight it? Was it a manoeuvre to gain time for a later fight? Or was it, as Emil Mazey believes, based on the hope that 'the company might be able to take over the Ford local from the inside'?[90]

The evidence points to Mazey's interpretation. As early as 1938 Homer Martin, the right-wing President of the UAW,

had been bargaining secretly with Harry Bennett, perhaps in an attempt by Ford to convince Martin, *in exchange for union recognition*, to lead the auto union back into the more conservative American Federation of Labor.[91]

Actually Martin did not have the influence to do so and was expelled from the union. In 1940 another attempt was made to use his services when, describing himself as an AFL organiser, he urged 3,000 black workers to break the strike. But it is the activities of Santo Perrone, a gangster who served six years for violating Prohibition laws in the Detroit area, which gives most support to Mazey's views.

In 1934 J.A.Fry, President of the Detroit Michigan Stove Co., employed Perrone to recruit strike-breakers and stop the unionisation of the plant. Mazey had succeeded in organising the factory while Perrone was imprisoned for illegally manufacturing whisky: on Perrone's return the union organisation disappeared. Perrone was important in other companies in Detroit, notably in Briggs Manufacturing. In the 1940s Briggs, Perrone and Melvin Bishop (a regional director of the UAW) seem to have made a deal which involved the intimidation of radical unionists, such as Mazey and his Socialist Workers Party followers. In March 1945 four members of Mazey's group were severely beaten; and soon after Perrone's son-in-law, Carl Ronda, received a scrap-hauling contract from Briggs, identical to that

Perrone had been granted by Michigan Stove in 1934. Despite pressure from the unions nothing was done by the Detroit police. Mazey commented:

> We [the UAW] believe that law enforcement agencies were not really interested in solving some of the crimes committed against our union because they were paid off by the organised rackets.[92]

Violence continued, including the shooting and wounding of Walter Reuther. The UAW hired Ralph Winstead and Herbert Blankerhern, former NLRB special investigators. Years later in 1957, just a few days before Winstead was due to use his massed information on the underworld at the UAW trial, his body was found in Lake St Clair. The cause of his death was never satisfactorily explained. Ironically the plot at Ford failed and the Ford Local 600 was controlled by the Communist Party.[93]

Although America was not officially involved in the Second World War until Pearl Harbor in December 1941, Roosevelt had already long been calling his country the 'arsenal of democracy'. Many of the trade-union leaders whose membership had been increasing through the Wagner Act were suggesting, particularly early in 1941, a no-strike pact. Although initially opposed to these ideas, with Germany's invasion of Russia in June of that year, leading Communist Party trade unionists became as dedicated as many more right-wing trade unionists to containing working-class militancy. This was their policy at the August 1941 conference of the UAW. At that time Walter Reuther, already a major figure in the union, although an opponent of communist and the other major left-wing tendencies in the union, was a strong supporter of the no-strike pledge. However,

> Many rank-and-filers opposed that plan, but in 1943 Reuther found a way to win back support. The communists announced their support for piecework, a means of incentive pay. Reuther, sensing that the rank and file was against piecework, which would tend to speed up the work rate, announced that he opposed the plan, and at the union convention at Buffalo in 1943, his proposal against piecework was passed.[94]

As a result 'Reuther emerged from the war years with his reputation as a militant intact'.[95] The massive confrontation with General Motors in 1945 resulting from Reuther's demand for a 30 per cent wage increase without a price increase seemed to confirm this.

Moreover the period from 1945 to 1946 saw 'American labor's greatest upsurge'. There were 41,750 strikes in 1945 involving 3,470,000 workers, and 4,985 in 1946 involving 4,660,000 workers (in the previous ten years the average annual number of strikes was 3,551 and the number of workers involved averaged 1,586,000). The disputes involved among others the United Auto Workers, the United Mineworkers, the International Longshoreman's Association, as well as lumber workers, glass workers, textile workers, oil workers, steelworkers and the railway brotherhoods.[96] There were general strikes in Lancaster, Pennsylvania, Stamford, Connecticut, Rochester, New York and Oakland California.[97] At the same time there was discussion about the need for a party like the British Labour Party which had just come to power. This was still thought by many American politicians and businessmen to be dangerously radical. In the 1948 presidential election ex-New Deal administrator Henry Wallace, supported by the Communist Party, only just missed UAW ratification, thereby losing the necessary working-class base; he still polled over a million votes. (He described himself as an 'American capitalist, a progressive Tory'.)

There was a real cause for concern over the political loyalties of the organised working class, particularly since Russia had been America's ally during the war. However the combined assault on anti-radical activities by the government, by the major political parties and by the right-wing trade-unionists in the context of the developing cold war policies of the Truman administration succeeded in negating any such potential. Although Truman had in 1945 been forced to abandon his plan to introduce conscription against the 'red threat', in 1947 he signed the anti-union and anti-radical Taft Hartley Act. In 1948 the 1940 Smith Act was used against leading Communists and in 1950 the McCarran 'Anti-Subversive Activities Act' was passed. Reuther's anti-Communist attacks in the UAW and in the CIO were becoming ever more clearly linked with these cold war policies. At the same time major companies, particularly General Motors, were beginning to recognise him as a reasonably acceptable trade-union leader. Charles P. Wilson, Chairman of General Motors, joined him on a Detroit citizens' committee so as to get to know him and they developed a liking for each other as the years passed. Two pro-business-unionism journalists said of one of his contracts with General Motors:

> The 1950 contract embellished Reuther's already considerable reputation within the labor movement and in the nation at large, as an imaginative union leader who could win major gains without strikes. *Fortune* summed up the UAW achievement: 'In the year beginning June, 1950, his auto workers got about 24 cents added to their basic hourly rates; there was not a single strike of consequence in the industry. Most labor leaders are accustomed to puffing and heaving, and sometimes striking, for the pennies per hour they get for their men, but Walter Reuther makes it look easy'.[98]

As Serrin points out in his study *The Company and the Union*, Reuther justified such faith, and the union's willingness to discipline wildcat strikers and to engage in ritualised conflict allowed for the removal of one of the manufacturers' greatest problems, unpredictable interference in the production process by the workers. He also continued his support for cold war policies, being at the founding conference for the CIA front, the Congress for Cultural Freedom, and later in 1966, by channelling $50,000 from the CIA to the weak European labour unions which were 'especially vulnerable to Communism'.[99] The changed political climate and the neutralisation of the radical potential in the union through men like Reuther made gangsters unnecessary. This, rather than 'a freak of coincidence' (as Whitty puts it), explains why the plan to extend gangster control from Briggs to Ford to Chryslers and then to industries in other states was not implemented. Indeed, since gangsters may attempt to 'muscle' their employers they are a poor substitute for compliant right-wing trade unionists. Their services no longer required, the underworld servants were disposed of.

> A Ford salvage official, tipped off by Herbert that the Perrone invasion was forthcoming and having learned that the Bennett regime was at the edge of collapse, took it upon himself to run Ronda and Perrone out of River Rouge. This stopped the Chrysler arrangement and would indicate that Bennett was pivotal in the plan's broader scope.[100]

The New York Docks

I have spent some time on the operations of syndicated crime in the Detroit area to show that Bell was wrong in saying

141

that labour rackets were limited to marginal industries. However, he himself admits one important exception – the 'racket ridden longshoremen'. He argues that racketeers were important in the New York Docks because they performed certain important functions. In New York Harbour the narrow piers and grid-iron street layout made congestion a continuous problem. The long waiting time for loading and unloading freight increased the costs to both the steamship companies and the truckers. From the point of view of the shipping companies the ideal situation was one where casual labour was in abundant supply, so allowing for speedy unloading and low wages. Such labour conditions were best guaranteed by a union that was racket-dominated, such as the International Longshoreman's Association (ILA). Besides the usual sweetheart contract, the racketeers benefited in other ways.

> Control of a union local means control of a pier, and control of the host of rackets that are spawned on the docks. A victorious clique has a number of concessions it can parcel out. These include bookmaking, loan-sharking, kickbacks for jobs, etc. ... But the biggest prize of all was the loading racket.[101]

Because of the long waits involved, drivers did not bring their own loaders but hired them at the pier. These could only be hired through the 'loading' bosses, who were union members and indeed dominated the ILA. They charged high prices for the privilege of using the labour that they controlled. With the institutionalisation of these bosses in a strong-arm organisation known as Varick Enterprises Inc., all truckers had to pay a tax per ton whether they used loaders or not, and if they were very short on time they could pay a 'hurry up' fee and go to the head of the line.

However, the rates were unpredictable, causing resentment among the truckers, who found it difficult to work out their costs accurately when charging customers. Consequently the truckers, led by Joseph Adelizzi, Managing Director of the Motor Carriers Association, brought pressure to bear and more standardised rates were worked out.

The truckers were reasonably happy, the steamship companies were happy. There was also a close political tie-up between the ILA and Tammany Hall; Joseph P. Ryan, who in 1943 had been made President for Life of the ILA, had political connections with businessman William J. McCormack who was 'one of the silent powers in Democratic politics',[102] and Mr Big on the waterfront. The ILA supported the Democrats and were in turn protected by them. These détentes nevertheless fail to explain the persistence of racketeer domination in New York. Instead Bell focuses on ecological factors.

> The real significance of the racket, for sociological investigation, is that 'loading' is to be found only in the New York waterfront. There has never been a loading racket in San Francisco, in New Orleans, in Baltimore or Philadelphia – the other major maritime ports in the US. There are many indigenous or historical factors to account for this lack, but the key fact is that the spatial arrangements of these other ports is such that loading never had a 'functional' significance. In all these ports, other than New York, there are direct railroad connections to the piers, so that transfer of cargoes is easily and quickly accomplished; nor is there in these ports the congested and choking narrow streets which in New York forced the trucks to wait...[103] How can one break this vicious cycle? One answer is the 'regularisation' of work...But is not enough. The matrix of the problem is the dilapidated physical condition of the port...and the fulcrum is still time.[104]

Bell is right to argue that a crucial difference between New York and the other docks is the congestion produced by the narrow piers and grid-iron streets. He is wrong, however, in arguing that racketeering was a necessary consequence of this.

A strong socialist union would have soon eliminated the racketeers and in America as a whole such socialist influence was a real possibility up until the late 1940s. In the case of the longshoremen there are additional reasons for arguing this. There was the precedent of the clean radical West Coast union, the International Longshoreman's and Warehouseman's Union. This had been formed in 1937 under the leadership of Harry Bridges when the Pacific seaboard longshoremen rejected the ILA-AFL and went into the CIO.[105] There was also the strong radical tradition in New York itself. One reason why events turned out as they did in New York was that dissidents were 'dealt with', by refusing them employment, a powerful weapon given the large numbers of casual workers, and by violence.

Bell admits that when in the thirties 'the Communists sought to gain a foothold among the Italian workers',[106] such rebellions were dealt with summarily. In 1939 Peter Panto, an 'insurgent leader of the longshoremen on the Brooklyn Docks',[107] was murdered by Albert Anastasia. 'Although a former killer for the mob, Allie Tannebaum, testified that Anastasia had personally supervised the killing, District Attorney William O'Dwyer unaccountably failed to press the indictments'.[108] In fact, he had intimated to Marcy Potter, a member of the Brooklyn-Queens Labor and Citizens Committee and of the American Labor Party, that he might do so if he received the support of the American Labor Party at the forthcoming elections.[109] Such support being refused he would gain nothing and possibly antagonise the syndicate if he were to prosecute. The canvassing of the ALP is yet another indication that socialist ideas were important in the dockland area.

Despite intimidation the influence of left-wingers increased. In 1945, the rank and file rejected one of J.P.Ryan's sweetheart agreements. The opposition was led by Local 791, pressurised 'by a rank-and-file committee in Brooklyn headed by a man named William E.Warren, but guided actually by the Communists'.[110] The men won their demands and returned to work. Ryan then expelled Warren from the union for allegedly not paying his dues. Later when he still reported for work he 'fell and hurt himself'. After exposure to such terrorising tactics and needing to earn a living, Warren not surprisingly repudiated his Communist associates.

During this period too there was a powerful New York socialist movement. This was made clear in evidence presented in the report of the Investigation of Communism in New York City Distributive Trades, June-August 1948. One witness, a department store executive, complained about massive demonstrations by the many left-wing unions. This certainly caused concern, for most of these unions were later 'investigated'. In fact in 1950-51 over a million trade unionists in 12 unions, *one fifth of its membership*, were expelled from the CIO. These unions included Bridges' ILWU, the International Fur and Leather Workers' Union, the United Electrical, Radio and Machine Workers and the American Communications Association.[111]

In 1953 because of growing internal dissension the ILA called a genuine strike. Faced by normal union demands the

144

steamship companies lost any advantages from their détente with the ILA. Ed Reid wrote at the time:

> Longshoremen working in a regularised port (decasualised and properly unionised) can earn more money over the year. In San Francisco the majority of longshoremen earn more than $3,500 a year. In New York the majority earn less than $2,500 a year.[112]

Bad publicity about the waterfront also made some attempt at a clean-up necessary. As a result, the AFL expelled the ILA in 1953, chartered a new union and the men were asked to vote for which they wanted to represent them. The ILA won by a narrow majority. Bell lists many reasons for this – including a distrust of the AFL union as a real alternative. Again he mentions, but underplays, the most important. 'Years of racket control...had eliminated the independent leadership among the men.'[113]

The political climate in America after seven years of McCarthyism and the cold war made the development of radical unionism unlikely then. I have shown that a radical potential existed; it will strengthen the argument if I demonstrate the awareness that existed of the relationship between why and how it was pre-empted. The clue to this is given in Ed Reid's work. He points out the effects of decasualisation of labour in Britain's dockland in 1946:

> Waterfront crime has been reduced, but frequent strikes have harrassed shipping in British ports. Since 1946, thirty-four dock strikes have closed ports in England and Scotland for periods up to forty-two days... Most were not authorised by the union. The British scheme for dock reform, therefore, seems hardly a solution for labour leaders in this country.[114]

Given the narrow piers, etc. tremendous economic and political power would be in the hands of workers who worked there. At city level this was recognised in 1950 by Governor Thomas E.Dewey, originally elected in 1942 on a racket-busting ticket, who sent this letter to J.P.Ryan, President of the ILA:

> Dear Joe,
>   I would surely be delighted to come to the annual affair of the Joseph R.Ryan Association on Saturday May 20th, if possible. As it happens, Mrs. Dewey and I have accepted an invitation to the marriage of Lewell Thomas's only son that weekend and we just can't possibly make it.

It is mighty nice of you to ask me and I wish you would give my regards to all the fine people at the dinner.

On behalf of the people of the entire state, I congratulate you and I thank you for what you have done to keep the Communists from getting control of the New York waterfront. Be assured that the entire machinery of the Government of New York State is behind you and your organisation in this determination.

With warm regards,
Sincerely yours,
Thomas E. Dewey.[115] [emphasis added]

There is also evidence of Federal acceptance of the racketeers. In 1941 rank-and-file members had begun a legal suit challenging the validity of wage agreements, alleging that true overtime had not been paid.

Their claim was upheld by the Wage and Hour Administrator, by seven different courts (including three US Circuit Courts of Appeal) and finally, in 1948, by the US Supreme Court which held that the longshore contracts violated the Wage and Hour law.[116]

The ILA and the steamship companies colluded to avoid the implications of this judgement, which included opening the books to public inspection, thus showing that frauds had been perpetrated against the Federal government during the war. When there was industrial action by the rank-and-file in August 1948 Truman slapped down an eighty-day Taft-Hartley injunction. In March 1949 a congressional bill reversed the Supreme Court decision. There was here a high degree of tacit government support for the 'working arrangements' between the corrupt union and the dockland bosses. Bell's inability to recognise this, despite the pointers to such a possibility to be found in his own essay, is symptomatic of his general position. He has such a strong antipathy to 'extreme' left-wing ideas that it produces a state of conceptual blindness. For Bell, like most bourgeois social scientists, men cannot rationally be revolutionary socialists and therefore to become so would not provide a meaningful solution to any of their problems.

6. Racketeering in an International Context

Earlier I pointed out that a marxist analysis of crime entailed an international dimension. Events within any society are affected to a greater or lesser extent by their political, social and cultural relationship with other countries. In any examination of the international context, care must be taken to deal with what is actually being done, by governments and by international corporations and agencies such as the International Monetary Fund, as well as what is presented by various governments as the rationale for their action. Thus in both Britain and America opposition to communist Russia has inspired much of their foreign policy *from 1917 until the present day*. Direct British intervention in Russia was only stopped by the threat of working-class political action and President Wilson sent American troops into Siberia to aid anti-bolshevik forces from 1918 to 1920.[117] During the 1920s and 1930s the anti-Russian policies continued although America was less fierce in this opposition than Britain. During the Second World War America concentrated against Japan, leaving Russia to bear the brunt of the war against Germany.

> From early 1941 until the Normandy landings of June 1944, the entire strength of the British Empire and Commonwealth engaged between two and eight divisions of the principal Axis power, Germany. During all but the first six months of the same period, the Soviet Union withstood, contained and eventually repulsed, an average of about 180 German divisions.[118]

It seems likely that the decision taken by Churchill and supported by Roosevelt not to open a second front until 1944 was politically motivated. ('Western experts expected a rapid capitulation of Russia before the German onslaught'.[119])

Kolko has shown that particularly from 1943 onwards the alliances on which the war was conducted were extremely complex. Britain, America and Russia were all fighting Germany. In addition, Britain and America wished to see Russia rendered ineffective as a world power and to limit the spread of the revolutionary anti-capitalist movements springing up all over Europe. At the same time America and Britain were competing for world mastery of capitalism.[120]

This hot and cold war context makes more comprehensible the Federal collusion in the maintenance of racketeer control of the waterfront already mentioned. In 1942:

> Accurate information on sailing dates and cargoes of ships leaving New York was reaching the cordon of German submarines which then virtually

controlled the Eastern seaboard and sank our and British shipping almost at will. At a meeting of the harrassed Naval Intelligence staff, at 90 Church Street, one day someone advanced the idea of enlisting the tightly organised New York-New Jersey dock underworld in the struggle. The Annapolis professional police officers saw the possibilities at once. No force could patrol the vulnerable piers and ships as effectively as the tough, alert long-shoremen, truckers and watchmen who knew every inch of them. The waterfront prostitutes and their pimps could be a counter-intelligence corps, if properly organised on the first order...There was only one man who had sufficient authority to solve the problem – and that was Lucky Luciano...Every few weeks a small group of naval officers in civilian clothes headed by his old friend and lawyer, Moses Polakoff, would go to visit him...The details are conjecture and always will be. In any case, the arrangement seems to have been effective. There was surprisingly little sabotage or any other trouble on the docks of the 3rd Naval District during the remainder of the war . . .[121]

In 1954 Luciano went before the Parole Board and because of his contribution to the war effort was granted parole and exiled for life.

Because of difficulties of corroboration and because of official secrecy, this story is contentious – on balance, though, the evidence seems strong. It is clear that rather than have a 'clean union' that might have communist sympathies – a possible solution to both problems since Russia was then at war with Germany – Federal authorities preferred to legitimate racketeer control of the docks. They were fighting the cold war during the Second World War, this time at home.

The connection with organised crime did not end there since Sicilian Americans and local Mafiosi were used by the Allies in their 1943 invasion of Italy. When the Allied armies landed:

The basic premise of American occupational planning prior to the conquest of Italy was to maintain existing governmental structures, laws, and even official personnel so long as they did not conflict with military needs or ultimate political objectives.[122]

Their appointment of well known Mafiosi as mayors all over Sicily[123] is also compatible with 'ultimate political objectives' their anti-socialist role in Italian politics being well known.[124] Since then the Mafiosi have justified such confidence by their dedicated opposition to socialism in any of its forms.[125] There is also evidence of Italian-American activity. Vito Genovese the New York mobster who had earlier escaped to Italy when under indictment for murder, worked 'as an unofficial adviser to the American military government'. A special agent for Military Intelligence arrested him when he was found to be a strong supporter of fascism and a black-marketeer. No help was received from the military authorities or the FBI and, indeed, when Genovese was brought back to America he was never tried for murder because of 'lack of witnesses'.[126] American cold war interests had helped create the organisation which was to be primarily responsible for smuggling heroin into that country for the next 20 years.

Cold war policies had a similar effect in France. In the late forties there was world-wide opposition to America's Marshall Plan, which was seen by many as part of the attempt to divide Europe and also to give direct aid in the fight against communism.

> Thus more than half the military and economic assistance to the French under the Marshall Plan and NATO was not to protect metropolitan France against the mythical soviet threat, but to restore her colonial control in Algeria and Vietnam.[127]

France at this time was riven by conflict between the working class who supported the communists and other left-wingers, and right-wingers like de Gaulle and his anti-communist party. In 1947 there was a massive general strike, eventually called off in December. The major confrontation in the struggle took place in Marseille and at that time:

> Victory in Marseille was essential to US Foreign Policy for a number of reasons. As one of the most important international ports in France, Marseille was a vital beach-head for Marshall Plan exports to Europe. Continued Communist control of its docks would threaten the efficiency of the Marshall plan and any future aid programmes. As the second largest city in France, continued Communist domination of the Marseille electorate would increase the chance that the Communist Party might win enough votes to form a national government...The CIA...sent agents and a psychological warfare team to Marseille, where they dealt directly with Corsican syndicate leaders through the Guerini brothers. The CIA's operatives supplied arms and money to Corsican gangs for assault on Communist picket lines and harassment of the important union officials. During the month-long strike the CIA's gangsters and the purged CRS police units murdered a number of striking workers and mauled the picket lines.[128]

In 1950 when Marseille dockers refused to move arms shipments for France's war in Indochina, the CIA moved again. This time, as well as the Guerinis another Corsican gangster, Pierre Ferri-Pisani, was paid to recruit an elite criminal terror squad to work in the docks. He received $15,000 from Irving Brown, then head of the AFL mission in Europe, money which he, in turn, received from Thomas Braden of the CIA.

The successful attack on communist control of the waterfront made Marseille wide open for the Corsican smugglers. Their most profitable commodity was heroin, refined in Marseille and then clandestinely exported to the United States. The CIA had helped build the French connection.

Yet another country sympathetic to gangsters, in part because of American foreign policy, was Cuba. From the time of America's intervention in the war between the nationalist movement in Cuba and her colonial master, Spain, the United States government abrogated to itself the right to veto Cuban governments. With massive US investments in the country, this meant that no left-wing government would be tolerated. From the first days of independence the governments were invariably corrupt, plundering the treasury and organising rigged lotteries. From 1933 until 1959 the dominant political figure was Batista; this was equally true whether he was bearing the title of President or in the background. He willingly adopted Meyer Lansky – America's most important gambling magnate – to set up operations in the 1930s and it was not long before Lansky owned most of Havana's casinos. His Miami connections stood him in good stead, for the Cubans had much of their capital invested in Miami, and Luciano was able to complete one of his routes for the shipping of heroin.[129] In the forties and fifties Lansky's interests in Cuba seem to have been seen to by the Santo Trafficantes, father and son

> As his father's financial representative, and ultimately Meyer Lansky's Santo Jr controlled much of Havana's tourist industry and became quite close to the pre-Castro dictator, Fulgencio Batista.[130]

In 1957 ten new lush gambling casinos were opened

> ...under the auspices of the Batista government, which had waived certain taxes, lent money, permitted professional gamblers to enter Cuba for two years as 'technicians' and presumably was taking a cut in the profits.[13]

This paradise was disturbed by the successful Cuban revolution of 1959:

Rumours regarding the abolition of gambling circulated throughout the island during the first days of the new government. Substance was given to these reports as notorious US racketeers – those who had not yet escaped – were rounded up by rebel troops for questioning.[132]

Although there was a small respite, gambling and the gamblers were banned from Cuba. However, they retained their connections with the prominent right-wing Cubans exiled in Cuba, as did pro-Batista politicians like Richard Nixon.

The final example of American government 'sponsorship' of gangsters again involves heroin, but in this case the intermingling of political corruption and cold war policies is far more naked. Southeast Asia – the major theatre of American military operations in the sixties and early seventies – has become the major supplier of heroin to the American market. It has done so because of America's military policies and, at least in part, because of CIA involvement with the transportation of opium in their own airline Air America.[133] In doing so they have followed the spirit of the British and French colonial adventurers. The former fought the Opium War of 1839-42 for the right to peddle the drug which had been decreed illegal in their main market, China. The French financed their administration in Indochina through opium sales and later helped finance their war against the liberation forces, as well as gaining political support from their allocation of the opium franchise. After the French pulled out there was a lull in the traffic until, in 1958, the American-supported Diem administration was faced with large-scale insurgency and so revived the opium trade with Laos to finance counter-insurgency operations. Faced with similar problems in 1965, Premier Ky's adviser, General Loan, used the same methods.

Saigon in South Vietnam and Bangkok in Thailand are the major distribution centres for the opium grown in Southeast Asia's 'Golden Triangle'. This stretches across 150,000 square miles of northeast Burma, northern Thailand and northern Laos. All of the countries involved have been subjects of the anti-communist policies of the major western powers, and ironically Saigon became the major exporter to the American and European markets.[134]

The CIA involvement in the propagation of a commodity that another governmental bureau was committed to fighting requires some explanation. It is possible that there has long been a combination of ignorance and a simple conflict of interest. Narcotics agents tended to concentrate on Europe but, when they did look to Laos, because of GI addiction 'investigations were blocked by the Laotian Government, the State Department and the CIA'.[135] It may be good for American foreign policy to allow the traffic in heroin but it is bad for the homeland if many of its middle-class youth are strung out. However, there may be more to the problem, as one black minister commented:

> Heroin and other drugs are seen by some blacks in the ghetto as the white man's way of exercising social control over ghetto dwellers. Every time there has been a major disturbance in a disadvantaged community, heroin has become readily available. Black leaders believe and rigidly accept the idea that the enemy places heroin in the community to prevent them from rising above their situation.[136]

I think that this tour of American foreign policy from the Second World War and over much of the globe must forestall the premature dismissal of such a view. It is a frightening possibility. It also provides a good theoretical terminus for this section since it started with internal political processes related to an international context, and so it ends.

7. Ruling-Class Opposition to Syndicated Crime

Labour Racketeering

In this attempt to undermine the conventional view that organised crime is an excrescence on the American body politic it may appear that I have taken too little account of the legislative and police assaults that it has suffered. So in this section these will be examined. The analysis in the previous section might seem to founder on governmental attitudes towards syndicated crime since the early 1950s. The Kefauver Commission (1951), the McClellan Commission (1959-60), the Landrum-Griffiths Act (1959), FBI activity and the Organised Crime Control Act (1970) all seem to indicate serious concern. Such concern is not totally unexpected since the underworld is a servant and will only be tolerated in so far as it is useful to the ruling class and it may always behave rashly. Nevertheless, an analysis of state action is itself illuminating.

The Kefauver Commission may have made a great public impact but no legislation followed. Despite its revelations syndicated crime remained strong. In the 1957 gathering of racketeers at Appalachia, N.Y. labour-racketeering was second only to gambling as the most common form of syndicate activity.[137]

In 1957, the McClellan Committee was appointed to investigate racketeering in the labour field. Its full title was the Select Committee on Improper Activities in Labor-Management Affairs. Its personnel was drawn from two other committees: the Permanent Sub-Committee on Investigations of the Committee on Government Investigations (Senators John L.McClellan, Democrat, Arkansas; Sam J.Ervin Jr, Democrat, North Carolina; Joseph R.McCarthy, Republican, Wisconsin; and Karl E.Mundt, Republican, South Dakota); and the Labor Sub-Committee on Labor and Public Welfare (Senators John F.Kennedy, Democrat, Massachussetts; Pat MacNamara, Democrat, Michigan; Irving Ives, Republican, New York; Barry Goldwater, Republican, Arizona). The high representation of Republicans and Southern Democrats is worth noting. This alone provided good reason for organised labour to be suspicious of this committee.[138] (During the hearings it became known that the righteous Senator Goldwater was a 'boon companion' of the labour-racketeer Willie Bioff.[139])

Although the Committee looked at illegal practices by certain managements (including Sears Roebuck, mentioned in relationship to Capone), it is best known for the clashes between the (late?) Teamsters' leader, Jimmy Hoffa and the chief counsel to the Committee, Robert F. Kennedy. On the evidence presented, there seems little doubt that Hoffa misappropriated union funds, was connected with many well-known racketeers such as Johnny Dioguardia, and had undisclosed business interests in the companies with which he dealt.[140] But John L.Lewis of the

Mineworkers said after the hearings: 'Mr Hoffa seems to be flourishing like a green bay tree. His members support him because he brings home the bacon to them, and they are interested in the bacon.'[141] Krislov, a disinterested observer, wrote that: 'Hoffa's successful contract negotiations seemed to far outweigh the effect of accusations of corruption.'[142]

In reality Hoffa seems to have taken the ideology of business unionism to its logical extreme. He was making the best of the capitalist system for himself and providing his members with good wages. However his racist outlook made him willing to set up paper locals in New York amongst black and Puerto Rican workers and later in opposition to Chavez's Mexican-American United Farm Workers. Such groups looked to the Kennedys for help and voted for them. That the Teamsters had been an AFL union was no coincidence for in previous years 'the AFL complained that the CIO was dominated by Communists, while the CIO complained the AFL was dominated by racketeers'[143]. Writing in 1958, Saposs pointed out that

> ...most of the former CIO unions are still dedicated to an ideal that tempers exclusive emphasis on immediate economic gains (old AFL unions of similar ideology have also vigorously and successfully resisted racketeering and underworld domination).[144]

Given Hoffa's successful business unionism, that another Teamster leader Harold Gibbons was criticised for being too militant,[145] and the amount of time the McClellan Committee spent investigating the 'clean' and more radical UAW, the Committee was clearly not just interested in corruption. Other legislation to deal with this already existed. In 1946 Truman had signed the notorious Hobbs Bill.

> This was ostensibly aimed at labor 'racketeers' particularly in the AFL teamsters union. The Act provided for fines up to $10,000 and 20 years imprisonment for strikers and pickets who might be convicted of 'racketeering', which in any way obstructs, delays or affects interstate commerce. The CIO called the anti-racketeering label on the Hobbs Bill a 'gross deception'. There was already an Anti-Racketeering Act in the federal statutes but its language specified that its provisions were not to apply to 'the payment of wages for bona fide employees' and it was not to be construed 'in such a manner as to impart, diminish, or in any manner affect the rights of bona fide labor organisations in lawfully carrying out the legitimate objects thereof'. The Hobbs Act excluded these safeguards.[146]

The *Interim Report* of the Committee (1958) focused on the sufferings of union members and the harm to the community caused by union corruption. The publicity surrounding its hearings and the experience of its personnel made it a natural resource for those who drew up a bill to 'regularise' union affairs.

McAdams has provided a detailed history of the legislation that was passed, the Labor-Management Reporting and Disclosure Act of 1959. He claims that this particular law was an unexpected product of the Eighty-sixth Congress. His book details the 'wheeling and dealing' that took place, and suggests that certain clauses slipped in almost by accident. The Act provided for government intervention in the affairs of unions to 'ensure democracy'. This was strongly opposed by the unions who recognised that such interference diminished their autonomy and freedom. These provisions can be seen to be a 'natural' outcome of the propaganda work of the McClellan Committee. However, Section 602 outlawing 'extortionate picketing', and Section 604 outlawing 'boycotts and recognition picketing' were both attacks on normal union practices. Joseph Loftus, in the *New York Times*, pointed out that the 'issues – boycotts, picketing, and Federal State jurisdiction (no man's land) – dwelt upon by the McClellan Report figure in the union-management power struggle'.[147] An irony of this Act was the hypocritical involvement of Ford executives in drafting such provisions, considering their own previous use of gangsters.[148]

An interesting feature of the McClellan Committee's *Interim Report* is its failure to discuss in detail the 'communist question'. Yet in volume ten of the proceedings of the Committee great stress had been placed on this. The Chairman in his introductory remarks was clear that:

> One of the interesting facts we expect to show is that at times the hoodlums used Communists or former Communists because they were excellently trained organisers and knew all the tricks to get membership.[149]

The only credible witness to this was Sam Zackman, an ex-communist who worked with Johnny Dioguardio.[150] But there was thought to be a greater danger, as Senator Mundt, Republican, South Dakota, put it:

> If we permit a situation to prevail whereby an unscrupulous cell of

powerful hoodlums can tie up our transportation systems and close down our factories we will be making a mockery of our entire programme of civilian defence...

Foreign Agents or Communist saboteurs by gaining control of this un-checked power to paralyse America could go far toward destroying our war potential and our capacity for self-defense. No multi-billion dollar programme of overseas military aid could offset the dangers we nourish at home by permitting conditions like these to prevail...

I would ask that our fellow citizens envision with me as these hearings proceed, what a quick transfer from the hands of a few hoodlums into the hands of a few Communists for thirty dirty pieces of silver could mean to the entire country and our capacity to defend ourselves.[151]

This outburst was occasioned by talk of a consultative council of transport unions to allow for coordinated industrial action. This would involve the ILA (corrupt union), the Teamsters (corrupt union), the railway brotherhoods (clean), the airline workers (clean), and Harry Bridges' West Coast Longshoremen (radical). Although Captain Bradley, the then President of the ILA, denied the possibility of an alliance with Harry Bridges[152], and although Hoffa expressed antipathy to the views of Harry Bridges[153], both secretly favoured such an alliance, as did Curran of the East Coast sailors. In the event it did not work out, in part because the propaganda against the idea scared off the other unions.[154] The fear of communists gaining control of transport was a major impetus for the Landrum-Griffiths Act. McAdams misses two vital indications of this. On 4 March 1958, President Eisenhower declared a 'National Defense Transportation Day' to emphasise the contribution of transport to national defence and in December of the same year a special report was made to the Congress. This was 'for official use only' and entitled 'Alliance of certain racketeers and communist dominated unions in the field of transportation as a threat to national security'.[155]

The Organised Crime Control Act (1970)

The Landrum-Griffiths Act, on investigation, seems primar-ily a weapon in the class struggle limiting union autonomy, militancy and solidarity as well as attacking possible left-wing tendencies. What of other legislation?

The evidence concerning state intervention against syndicated crime has shown that when the latter is functional in protecting American *capitalism* it is used; when it becomes dangerous it is attacked; for example in the case of military installations.[156] The liberal claim that syndicated crime is in some sense un-American is unconvincing, as is that of 'cynics' who say that it benefits or harms everybody equally. Csiscery has recently shown how top politicians are involved with syndicated crime. Thomas E.Dewey, racket-buster of New York, 'Will Wilson', general of the Justice Department's 'war' on crime from 1969-71, and Richard Nixon are all cited. The possible involvement of Nixon, syndicated gambling and vice, and Cuba's Batista regime once again provides an international dimension.[157] Given these connections it is no surprise to find that the Organised Crime Control Act (1970) is aimed at political radicals.

The Act's preamble waxes indignant over the extent, dangers, and immunity of organised crime. It sets out to combat these by having provision 'for, among other things, the creation of additional special grand juries, the admissibility of illegally obtained evidence', and the legal framework for extending the prison sentences of 'dangerous individuals' long beyond the normal prison sentence for a specific offence. It alters the 'immunity' granted to those who testify (from 'absolute' to a more limited 'use' immunity) and it further extends the power of the FBI.[158] Without wishing to go into great detail, I will briefly comment on Title 10, Dangerous Special Offenders. This section provides for the incarceration of an individual convicted of a felony for up to 25 years if he is determined by the court to be a 'dangerous special offender'. The court in this case means that the judge alone decides after the defendant has been found guilty of this offence. There are three possible grounds for such a judgement. They are if he is a defendant who:

1.   has been convicted of 2 or more offences punishable by death or imprisonment of more than one year, one of which has occurred within the last 5 years and for one of which he has been imprisoned.
or
2.   has committed the present felony as a part of a criminal pattern of conduct which 'constituted a substantial source of his income, and in which he manifested a precise skill or expertise'.
or
3.   has committed the felony as part of a *conspiracy* with three or more to 'engage in a pattern of conduct criminal under applicable law

157

and played some kind of active role, or used force or bribes in all or part of such conspiracy.[159]

Using criteria 1) and 3) most black militants and many white radicals would be liable for classification as Dangerous Special Offenders. The high risk of arrest experienced by all poor black people, the degree of state harassment of members or organisations such as the Black Panthers on the one hand, and, on the other, the possibility of conviction for narcotic offences of white militants recruited from a counter-culture which considers such a drug normal would see to that. The conspiracy provision is so flexible and extensible as to include almost any criminal offence. The minutes of evidence of those arguing for the law showed that they were aware of this. Moreover, the kind of 'force' that they had in mind was indicated by Title 11, 'Regulations of Explosives'. The Weathermen, the bank burners and other violently inclined opponents of capitalism were the major concern.[160] Once again state action cannot be taken at its face value. There is little evidence of any real concern over organised crime and this makes sense since it is no kind of threat to the world-wide power of American corporate capital.

8. Conclusion

What if the habits, problems, secrets, and unconscious motivations of the wealthy and powerful were daily scrutinised by a thousand systematic researchers, were hourly pried into, analysed and cross referenced, tabulated and published . . . ?[161]

Within sociology, and particularly within criminology, the serious study of the state and its agents and of the activities of the ruling class is virtually non-existent. A start has been made by scholars like Poulantzas and Miliband, but nevertheless most of what has been written has been administratively oriented or meritocratic in its inspiration. On the other hand, endless surveys and reports have been compiled on crime, racial disturbance, working-class militancy, drug 'abuse', etc. This book has also been concerned with crime, but in a different way. In it I have looked at the state, the ruling class and organised crime and have described the criminal conspiracy so often tying them together during this century. The intention in using a marxist approach has been to rescue the study of organised crime from the moralising empiricism of journalists and the political naivety of corporate liberals. By relating the varying fortunes of gangsters to the needs of the ruling class, the subordinate status of the former has become clear as has the need for an analysis of the mode of production of which the ruling class is an element. Only by understanding the development of monopoly capitalism within a world context is it possible to make sense of the development of syndicated crime in American and other countries. Furthermore, the distance between rhetoric and action becomes manifest when contrasting the publicly stated purpose of legislation and the actual targets in mind when it was framed and implemented.

The material in Parts 2 and 3 of this book shows that the most important practitioners of 'organised crime' within a national and international context are not the Capones, Lanskys or Lucianos of the world but the American corporations and their agent, the American state. However, whilst this may be true, much more work is needed on this topic. We know that many of the major American fortunes were made illegally (Russell Sage, for example, made his money from criminal fraud and then set up a foundation which sponsored studies of crime in the New York and Pittsburgh slums[162]). Again many British fortunes have been built on the terrorisation of colonial peoples as earlier the aristocracy had become rich through forced enclosures. But we do not have enough detailed work on either the present activities or the growth of the major corporations. The same, of course, applies to the repressive apparatus of the state. (Police violence in Britain during the General Strike and against the Hunger Marchers has almost been forgotten and is rarely mentioned in academic texts.)

Part 3 of this book is only indicative, more in the nature of development of a theoretical framework for analysing the problem than a completed piece of work in itself. One topic certainly worth investigating is the relationship between the American political parties and organised crime. A number of writers have already pointed to the strong evidence linking ex-President Nixon with organised crime, so it seems fitting to end with a quotation from him:

The organised criminal relies on physical terror and psychological intimidation, on economic retaliation and political bribery, on citizens' indifference and government acquiescence. He corrupts our governing institutions and subverts our democratic processes.[163] – Richard Nixon, 24 April 1969.

Notes

1. Bruce J.Cohen (ed.), *Crime in America*, Ithaca: Peacock 1970, p.299.
2. James Volz and Peter Bridge, *The Mafia Talks*, Greenwich: Fawcett Books 1969.
3. Ramsay Clarke, *Crime in America*, New York: Pocketbooks 1971, p.65.
4. American Friends Service Committee, *Struggle for Justice*, New York: Hill & Wang 1971, p.122; Alan Wolfe, *The Seamy Side of Democracy*, New York: McKay 1973, p.108.
5. Frank Pearce, 'Crime, Corporations and the American Social Order' in Ian Taylor and Laurie Taylor (eds.), *Politics and Deviance*, Harmondsworth: Penguin 1973.
6. Peter Maas, *The Canary that Sang: The Valachi Papers*, London: Panther Books 1970.
7. Donald R.Cressey, *Theft of the Nation: The Structure and Operations of Organised Crime in America*, New York: Harper & Row 1969, p.21. See also Donald R.Cressey, *Criminal Organisation*, London: Heinemann 1972.
8. Donald R.Cressey, *op.cit.*, 1969, pp.x-xi.
9. Joe L.Albini, *The American Mafia: Genesis of a Legend*, New York: Appleton-Century-Crofts 1971, p.47; I find another definition more appealing if less precise – a racket is 'any scheme by which human parasites graft themselves upon and live, by the industry of others, maintaining their hold by intimidation, force and terrorism', H.Hostetner quoted in Andrew Sinclair, *Prohibition: Era of Excess*, London 1965, p.238.
10. John Kobler, *Capone: The Life and World of Al Capone*, London: Michael Joseph 1971, p.87.
11. Daniel Bell, *The End of Ideology*, New York: Free Press 1960, p.147.
12. Peter Maas, *op.cit.*; Daniel Bell, *op.cit.*; B.B.Turkus and Sid Feder, *Murder Inc.*, New York: Harrar, Strauss & Gudhay, excerpted in Gus Tyler (ed.), *Organised Crime in America*, Michigan: Ann Arbor Paperbacks 1967. Wherever books have been excerpted in this volume page numbers refer also to this volume. Ted Poston, 'The Numbers Racket', *New York Post*, February 29-March 10 1960, excerpted in Gus Tyler, *op.cit.*
13. Francis A.Ianni, *A Family Business*, London: Routledge & Kegan Paul 1972.
14. B.B.Turkus, *op.cit.*
15. Daniel Bell, *op.cit.*
16. Daniel Glaser, *The Effectiveness of a Prison and Parole System*, Indianapolis: Bobbs-Merill 1964.
17. See Francis A.Ianni, *op.cit.*, and J.Kobler, *op.cit.*
18. Murray Kempton, 'Crime Does Not Pay', *New York Review of Books*, 11 September 1969.
19. John A.Gardiner and David J.Olson, 'Wincanton: The Politics of Corruption',

in William J.Chambliss(ed.), *Crime and the Legal Process*, McGraw-Hill 1969, p.134.

20. See Peter Nyden, 'Coal Miners, Their Union and Capital', *Science and Society*, pp.211-216.

21. Andrew Sinclair, *op-cit.*, p. 145.

22. See particularly James Weinstein, *The Decline of Socialism in America*, New York: Monthly Review Press 1967, and David W.Eakins and James Weinstein (eds.), *For A New America: Essays in History and Politics from 'Studies on the Left', 1959-1967*, New York: Random House 1970.

23. William Preston, *Aliens and Dissenters*, New York: Harper & Row 1966, and Herbert B.Ehrmann, *The Case that Will Not Die: Commonwealth vs. Sacco and Vanzetti*, London: W.H.Allen 1970.

24. Estes Kefauver, *Crime in America*, London: Gollancz 1952, pp.236-54.

25. *Internal Security Act of 1950*, 81st Congress, 2nd Sess., ch.1024, 23 September 1950.

26. However, see the comments in JOEY with D.Fisher, *Killer: Autobiography of 'Joey' A Professional Murderer*, London: W.H.Allen 1973. See also Hank Messick on the National Crime Commission and the Mafia. He writes: 'The author has maintained for years that if every member of the Mafia (or La Cosa Nostra) were jailed tomorrow, organised crime would be just as powerful as ever...' (Hank Messick, *Lansky*, Robert Hale 1973, p.8). Very tellingly he reports that: 'a high ranking justice official once explained to the author the decision to call the Mafia 'La Cosa Nostra'. 'Hoover', he said, 'could have called the Mafia the YWCA if he had wanted to; all Kennedy wanted to do was get him and his great organisation into battle.' When asked why the emphasis on the Mafia instead of the national crime syndicate the official said, 'The Mafia was small and handy.' The feeling was the American people would buy it with its family relations and blood oaths a lot quicker than they could understand the complex syndicate.' *(ibid., p.68)*.

27. See Gerald Csiscery, 'Nixon and the Mafia', *Sundance*, San Francisco, November-December 1972.

28. Daniel Bell, *op.cit.*, p.146.

29. *ibid.*, p.131.

30. James Weinstein, *op.cit.*, 1967, p.327.

31. John M.Allswang, *A House for All Peoples*, Lexington: University Press of Kentucky 1971.

32. John Kobler, *op.cit.*, p.203.

33. *ibid.*, p.199.

34. Daniel P.Moynihan, 'The Private Government of Crime', *The Reporter*, Vol.25, no.1, 1961, reprinted in Bruce J.Cohen (ed.), *Crime in America*, Peacock 1970, p.326.

35. Donald R.Cressey, *op.cit.*, p.75.

36. George Lundbergh, *The Rich and the Superrich*, New York: Bantam Books, 1968, p.119; however Francis A.Ianni, *op.cit.*, p.90, estimates that his New York 'Family' may be worth $15 million.

37. Francis A.Ianni, *op.cit.*, pp.87-107.

38. Robert B.Nye and James F.Morpurgo, *The Growth of the USA*, Harmondsworth: Penguin 1970, p.687.

39. George Lundbergh, *op.cit.*, p.119.

40. Kenneth Allsop, *The Bootleggers*, London: Arrow Books 1970, p.75.

41. John Landesco, *Organised Crime in Chicago: Part III of the Illinois Crime Survey 1929*, Chicago: University of Chicago Press, 1968; see also John Kobler, *op.cit.*, p.203.

42. Virgil Peterson, *Barbarians in Our Midst*, New York : Little Brown 1952, excerpted in Gus Tyler, *op.cit.*, p.160.

43. John Kobler, *op.cit.*, p.208.

44. Andrew Sinclair, *op.cit.*, p.107.

45. *ibid.*, pp.110-14.

46. Anthony Platt, *The Child Savers*, Chicago : University of Chicago Press 1969, and Anthony Platt, 'The Triumph of Benevolence', cyclostyled.

47. Kenneth Allsop, *op.cit.*, p.279.

48. *ibid.*, pp.80-81.

49. Claud Cockburn, *I Claud ... the Autobiography of Claud Cockburn*, Harmondsworth : Penguin 1967, pp.118-19.

50. William Preston, *op.cit.*, p.134.

51. See particularly James Weinstein, *op.cit.*, 1967, but also Jeremy Brecher, *Strike*, San Francisco : Straight Arrow Books 1972.

52. Alan Wolfe, *op.cit.*, pp.26-9.

53. William Z.Foster, *American Trade Unionism*, New York : International Publishers 1947, p.82.

54. John Williamson, *Dangerous Scot : The Life and Work of an American Undesirable*, New York : International Publishers 1969.

55. John Landesco, *op.cit.*, p.134.

56. John Kobler, *op.cit.*, p.266.

58. John M. Allswang, *op.cit.*, p.179.

59. Kenneth Allsop, *op.cit.*, p.338.

60. *ibid.*, p.332.

61. Andrew Sinclair, *op.cit.*, p.362.

62. Todd Gitlin, 'Local Pluralism as Theory and Ideology', in Hans P.Dreitzel (ed.), *Recent Sociology*, no.1, New York : Macmillan 1969; bearing in mind M.Banfield, *Political Influence*, New York : Free Press 1961 and Mike Royko, *Boss : Richard J.Daley of Chicago*, London : Paladin 1971.

63. See note 23.

64. Donald Cressey, *op.cit.*, 1972, p.83.

65. John Landesco, *op.cit.*, pp.107-47.

66. John Kobler, *op.cit.*, pp.231-3.

67. Gus Tyler, *op.cit.*, p.207.

68. Daniel Bell, *op.cit.*, p.176; see also Walter Lippmann, *op.cit.*, pp.58-69.

69. Roger Touhy, *The Stolen Years*, Pennington Press 1959, excerpted as 'The Labor Stakes and I' in Gus Tyler, *op.cit.* p.193; see also G. Tyler, *op.cit.*, pp.189-93, 197-205.

70. From the *Final Report*, Select Committee on Improper Activities in the Labor and Management Field, US Senate 1960, excerpted in Gus Tyler, *op.cit.*, p.32.

71. Daniel Bell, *op.cit.*, pp.68-9.

72. Tony Woodiwiss, 'Law, Labour and the State in the United States', in Mike Hayes and Frank Pearce (eds.), *Crime, Politics and the State*, London : Routledge & Kegan Paul 1976.

73. Brad Wiley, 'The Myth of New Deal Reform', cyclostyled.

74. *ibid.*, p.330. Thurman Arnold, a major New Deal philosopher, said the following in his book *The Symbols of Government :* 'The writer has faith that a new public attitude towards the ideals of law and economics is slowly appearing to create an atmosphere where the fanatical alignments between opposing political principles may disappear and a competent, practical, opportunisitic governing

162

class may rise to power...'; quoted in Howard Zinn, *The Politics of History*, Boston: Beacon Press 1970, p.121.

75. Richard Hofstadter, *op.cit.*, p.329.

76. Cited in Irving Bernstein, *Turbulent Years: a History of the American Worker 1933-1941*, Boston: Houghton Mifflin 1970, p.171.

77. Ronald Radosh, 'The Corporate Ideology of American Labor Leaders from Gompers to Hillman', originally published in *Studies on the Left*, Vol.6, no.6, November-December 1966, reprinted in David Eakins and James Weinstein (eds.), *op.cit.*

78. Quoted in Stuart Ewan, 'Advertising, Selling the System', *Radical America*, Vol.3, May-June 1969, reprinted in Milton Mankoff, *The Poverty of Progress*, New York: Holt, Rinehart & Winston 1972, p.436.

79. Brad Wiley, 'The Myth of New Deal Reformers', in *Corporations and Government*, p.133.

80. Karsten Struhl, 'From Civil Disobedience to Revolution', unpublished paper, Department of Philosophy, Long Island University.

81. Ovid Demaris, *op.cit.*, p.27.

82. Malcolm Johnson, *Crime on the Labor Front*, New York: McGraw-Hill 1950, reprinted in Gus Tyler, *op.cit.*, p.202.

83. *ibid.*, pp.203-5.

84. Staughton Lynd, 'The Possibility of Radicalism in the Early 1930s; The Case of Steel', in *Radical America*, Vol.2, no.6, November-December 1972.

85. See William Linder, 'The Great Flint Sit-Down Strike Against General Motors 1936-1937', *Solidarity* Pamphlet no.31, London 1969, p.5 and Irving Howe and B.J. Widick, *The UAW and Walther Reuther*, New York: Random House 1949, p.31.

86. William Linder, *op.cit.*, p.8.

87. There is a discussion of the general wave of sit-down strikes including this one in Jeremy Brecher, *op.cit.*

88. Irving Howe and B.J. Widick, *op.cit.*, p.92.

89. *ibid.* p.105.

90. *ibid.* p.105.

91. William Sherrin, *The Company and the Union*, New York: Knopf 1973, p.128.

92. Michael D. Whittey, 'The United Auto Workers Face Detroit's Underworld', *Criminology*, Vol.8, no.2, August 1970, p.132.

93. Irving Howe and B.J. Widick, *op.cit.*, p.157.

94. William Sherrin, *op.cit.*, p.135.

95. *ibid.*

96. Art Preis, *Labor's Giant Step*, New York: Pathfinder Press 1972, pp.xi, 283.

97. Jeremy Brecher, *op.cit.*, p.229.

98. F. Cormer and W.J. Eaton, *Reuther*, Englewood Cliffs: Prentice-Hall 1970, p.299.

99. See Christopher Lasch, *The Agony of the American Left*, Harmondsworth: Penguin 1973, p.65 and William Sherrin, *op.cit.*, p.147.

100. Michael D. Whitty, *op.cit.*, pp.141-2.

101. Daniel Bell, *op.cit.*, p.183.

102. *ibid.*, p.194.

103. *ibid.*, p.187.

104. *ibid.*, p.208.

105. Clarence P. Larrowe, *Harry Bridges: The Rise and Fall of Radical Labor* *in the USA*, New York: Lawrence Hill 1972, p.126. For a trotskyist assessment of Bridges see Ed Harris, 'The Trouble with Harry Bridges', *International Socialist*, September 1973, Vol.34, no.8.

106. Daniel Bell, *op.cit.*, p.197.

107. *ibid.*, p.192.

108. *ibid.*

109. Ed Reid, *The Shame of New York*, London: Gollancz 1954, pp.209-11.

110. Daniel Bell, *op.cit.*, p.198.

111. Clarence P. Larrowe, *op.cit.*, p.323.

112. Ed Reid, *op.cit.*, p.155.

113. Daniel Bell, *op.cit.*, p.205.

114. Ed Reid, *op.cit.*, p.156.

115. Quoted in Allen Raymond, *Waterfront Priest*, New York: Holt, Rinehart & Winston 1955, and excerpted in Gus Tyler, *op.cit.*, p.317.

116. Daniel Bell, *op.cit.*, p.208.

117. See William A. Williams, 'American Intervention in Russia: 1917-20', in David Horowitz (ed.), *Containment and Revolution*, London: Blond 1967.

118. John Baggueley, 'The World War and the Cold War', in D. Horowitz, *op.cit.*, 1967.

119. David Horowitz, *Empire and Revolution*, New York: Vintage 1969, p.180.

120. Gabriel Kolko, *The Politics of War: Allied Diplomacy and the World Crisis of 1943-1945*, London: Weidenfield & Nicolson 1969.

121. Francis Sondern, *Brotherhood of Evil*, London: Gollancz 1959, excerpted in Gus Tyler, *op.cit.*, pp.309-11. See also Estes Kefauver, *op.cit.*, pp.36-8.

122. Gabriel Kolko, *op.cit.*, p.69.

123. Norman Lewis, *The Honoured Society: The Mafia Conspiracy Observed*, Harmondsworth: Penguin 1967, p.19.

124. Joe L. Albini, *op.cit.*, p.83.

125. *ibid.*, p.139 and Norman Lewis, *op.cit.*, pp.145-7. See also Michele Pantaleone, *The Mafia and Politics*.

126. Peter Maas, *op.cit.*, pp.135-9.

127. David Horowitz, *op.cit.*, 1969, p.91.

128. W. McCoy, *The Politics of Heroin in South East Asia*, New York: Harper & Row 1972, pp.44-6. See also 'Footnotes', *Private Eye*, 11 April 1969.

129. See R. Scheer and M. Zeitlin, *Cuba: An American Tragedy*, Harmondsworth: Penguin 1964, p.29; Alfred W. McCoy, *op.cit.*, p.25; and Hank Messick, *op.cit.*

130. Alfred McCoy, *op.cit.*, p.27.

131. *Hispanic American Report*, Vol.10, no.12, December 1957, p.663.

132. *Hispanic American Report*, Vol.12, no.1, January 1959.

133. Alfred McCoy, *op.cit.*, p.247.

134. *ibid.*, p.150.

135. *ibid.*, p.350.

136. James H. McMearn, 'Radical and Racial Perspectives on the Heroin Problem', in David E. Smith and George R. Gay, *It's So Good Don't Even Try It Once: Heroin in Perspective*, Englewood Cliffs: Prentice-Hall 1972, p.123.

137. Joe L. Albini, *op.cit.*, pp.248-9.

138. Sidney Peck, *Rank and File Leader*, New Haven: College and University Press 1963.

139. Ed Reid and Ovid Demaris, *The Green Felt Jungle: The Truth about Las Vegas*, London: Heinemann 1965, p.42.

140. United States Senate, Select Committee on Improper Activities in the Labor and Management Field, *Interim Report*, 1958, pp.5267-273.

164

141. Andrew K. McAdams, *Power and Politics in Labor Legislation*, New York: Columbia University Press 1964, p.137.

142. S. Krislov, 'The Hoffa Case: The Criminal Trial and Process of Interest Group Leadership Selection', in Theodore L. Becker (ed.), *Political Trials*, New York: Bobbs-Merrill 1971.

143. John B. Martin, *Jimmy Hoffa's Hot*, Greenwich: Fawcett Publications 1959, p.15.

144. David J. Saposs, 'Labor Racketeering, Evolution and Solution', *Social Research*, Vol.25, Autumn 1958.

145. John B. Martin, *op. cit.*, p.100.

146. Art Preis, *op. cit.*, p.293.

147. Quoted in Andrew K. McAdams, *op. cit.*, p.197.

148. *ibid.*, p.192.

149. United States Senate Select Committee on Improper Activities in the Labor and Management Field, 1957, Vol.10, p.3592.

150. *ibid.*, p.3663.

151. *ibid.*, p.3595. (See also pp.3599-600.)

152. *ibid.*, p.4800.

153. *ibid.*, p.5108.

154. Daniel Bell, *op. cit.*, p.206; see also C. P. Larrowe, *op. cit.*, p.361.

155. 85th Congress, 2nd Session, December 17, 1958, ii-41p.

156. For racketeering and military installations see: United States House of Representatives, Special Subcommittee of the Committee on Government Operations and Education and Labor, 1953, *Hearings*, 'Special Subcommittee on Strikes and Racketeering in the Kansas City Area'; see also its 'Special Subcommittee on Strikes and Racketeering in the Detroit Area'. See also United States House of Representatives, Special Subcommittee of the Committee on Education and Labor, *Hearings*, 1948.

157. Gerald Csiscery, *op. cit.*, pp.68, 36-42.

158. Joan Roach, 'Conspiracy Law in the USA', unpublished paper for Sociology Department, California State University at Los Angeles, 1971, p.19.

159. United States: Public Law 91-452 – October 14, 1970, *An Act Relating to the Control of Organised Crime in the United States*.

160. On the Weathermen see Harold Jacobs (ed.), *Weathermen*, Berkeley: Ramparts Press 1970, and Paul Walton, 'The Case of the Weathermen: Social Reaction and Radical Commitment', in Ian Taylor and Laurie Taylor (eds.), *op. cit.*

161. Martin Nicolaus, text of a speech delivered at the ASA Convention, 26 August 1968. Reprinted in Larry T. Reynolds and Janice M. Reynolds, *The Sociology of Sociology*, New York: David McKay 1970, p.277.

162. 'Gustavus Myers in his book *History of the Great American Fortunes* refers to the incident in which Russell Sage and his business partners planned and executed a swindle of their creditors in Milwaukee with the ultimate irony being Sage himself hoodwinking his own partners out of their profit from the swindle. Closer to the traditional conception of racketeering is Myers' appraisal of Cornelius Vanderbilt's method of building his fortune which included forms of blackmail, theft and extortion.' Joe Albini, *op. cit.*, p.31.

163. Quoted in Gerald Csiscery, *op. cit.*, p.68.

Index

Martin Shaw

Marxism and Social Science
the roots of social knowledge

Martin Shaw argues that the crisis of the social sciences is not simply one of intellectual direction. It grows from the social sciences' roots in the industrial, educational and ideological systems of capitalist society discussed in this book. The solutions are not just theoretical – theory must be related to practice, within academic institutions as well as in the wider class struggle.

A companion volume to *Marxism versus Sociology: a guide to reading*, also by Martin Shaw.

Martin Shaw

Marxism versus Sociology:
a guide to reading

A companion volume to *Marxism and Social Science*, this guide is intended to aid students in the sociology departments of colleges and universities to work towards and within the tradition of marxism.

It provides an outline of a marxist critique together with an annotated reading list covering sociological theory and method; global perspectives on industrialisation, underdevelopment and comparative social structures; and elements of social structure – stratification, industrial and political sociology, sociology of knowledge, welfare, religion, culture and more.

Michael Kidron

Capitalism and Theory

A collection of interlocking essays about the permanent arms economy, and about marxism.

'Waste: US 1970' considers Marx's view on productive and unproductive labour and measures the size of the American productive economy.

'Black Reformism: the Theory of Unequal Exchange' is the first major critique in English of the theory of trade imperialism. It also covers the marxist theory of wages and the centralisation of capital.

Other essays in 'Capitalism and Theory' deal with Marx's theory of value, Russian state capitalism, Lenin's theory of imperialism, China, and the link between economic development in backward countries and revolution in the developed capitalist world.

Available from

Pluto Press
Unit 10 Spencer Court, 7 Chalcot Road,
London NW1 8LH

Complete list of
Pluto books and pamphlets
available on request